Contents

Seattle bootlegger Roy Olmstead and his wife, Elise ("Elsie"). By 1926, federal and local agents had crippled Olmstead's booze business, and he was fighting liquor charges at a precedent-setting criminal trial. *SEATTLE POST INTELLIGENCER* COLLECTION, MUSEUM OF HISTORY AND INDUSTRY

Prologue

LIQUOR DELIVERY MAN JOHNNY EARL *was still running on adrenalin after his escape from Prohibition agent "Two-Gun" James Johnson when he called dispatcher John McLean at the Seattle liquor ring's Henry Building phone exchange.*

"They got that load," Earl panted.

"The hell they did—who?" the asthmatic McLean wheezed.

"The federals."

"How'd it happen?"

"Jim Johnson came in the alley and took a shot at Phil and caught Berg. Phil and I got away. I jumped in a taxi and went to the lakefront and then on to the plant."

Minutes later, McLean rang Roy Olmstead. "Two-Gun

Johnson got a load up behind the A-1 [the A-1 Hotel, the delivery destination]. He got Berg and one of the cars; Earl and Phil got away."

Olmstead was his usual unflappable self. "Tell the boys to be mighty careful and hang pretty close together the rest of the day, and only deliver what orders they have."

The next morning, Johnny Earl was watching poolroom action inside Paul Hyner's cigar store on Third when he spotted Johnson. Earl turned and made a dash for it. He was on the sidewalk when Two-Gun stepped through the doorway, pulling his revolver.

"Run from me, will you, you bastard!" Johnson bawled, levelling his gun.

Crack! Pedestrians ducked and scattered. Johnny Earl collapsed to the pavement, clutching his thigh.

In Seattle's whisky war, Two-Gun's shoot-first-ask-questions-later reputation remained intact, and the reputation of Seattle's number-one bootlegger as untouchable had just taken another knock.

1

The Dawn of Dry BC

LIKE ALMOST EVERYONE ELSE IN Vancouver, Rogers Building barbers had been speculating on the upcoming 1916 election-day suffrage and prohibition referenda. But as scissors snipped and razors scraped inside the ornate emporium (the 18-chair facility with plate-glass mirrors and marble columns was much more than a mere barbershop), what dominated the conversation wasn't women's voting rights; it was liquor. While customers talked about prohibition, most barbers kept their ears open and mouths shut on "dry" and "wet" issues.

It made sense that many women were campaigning to end the making and selling of liquor. As Manitoba activist Nellie McClung had said, "We women have had nothing to do with the liquor business except to pay the price." That price was paid daily in pain and pride inside thousands of homes as drunken husbands battered wives while children went hungry because Daddy drank his paycheque away in a saloon. In spite of that, men were the only ones eligible to vote on the fate of the BC government—and liquor.

On September 14, 1916, men tossed Billy Bowser's scandalized Conservatives out and brought in Baptist Harlan Brewster's Liberals. Men decided to finally grant women the vote and, with a perverse blend of righteousness and patriotism, to outlaw saloons and the booze most enjoyed so much.

Roger's Building barbers had a personal connection with the struggle over drink that went beyond their taste for it. Jonathan Rogers, the builder and owner of the new downtown landmark, was one of prohibition's chief architects. Just as the completion of the majestic 10-storey building on the corner of Pender and Granville Streets had been a triumph for the pioneer Vancouver builder, so was the province's Prohibition Act. Rogers enjoyed enormous influence as city alderman and chair of both the Board of Trade and Parks Board. Much of what wealthy Rogers and his wife Elizabeth did, including helping to found the Vancouver Art Gallery and Vancouver Symphony, they did to better the lives of others. Rogers likely regarded this as his civic duty. Moreover, as a good Methodist, Rogers regarded prohibition support as his moral and spiritual duty as well. Rogers helped organize the People's Prohibition Association (PPA) and was elected

Vancouver builder Jonathan Rogers was an ideal choice for president of BC's Peoples Prohibition Association. CITY OF VANCOUVER ARCHIVES AM54-S4

its first president. He then provided the PPA with free office space in his building. After a year of hard lobbying for a prohibition referendum, Rogers was rewarded with a dry vote.

Walking into his Hastings Street office on BC's first dry morning, fellow Methodist and PPA member John Nelson was feeling mighty pleased, too. As the *Vancouver Daily World*'s new owner and editor, Nelson had turned the newspaper into a mighty weapon of the whisky wars. On the eve of the referendum, Nelson urged his readers, "Let your vote tomorrow be on the side of . . . the Mother and the Boy against the Saloon, the Brothel and the Distiller's profits."

Nelson had emphasized the need for BC people to unite in the war effort. The war Nelson referred to was not the one being fought by the province's wets and drys, but the one being fought in Flanders by over 40,000 uniformed BC men. Distillers and brewers, Nelson declared, had no business using valuable foodstuffs to manufacture intoxicants when British Columbians were fighting and dying in the mud of Passchendaele, Belgium. As workers abandoned farm fields for Flanders Fields, fears of food shortages loomed. The Canada Food Board advised BC residents to avoid wheat-based breakfast foods and to have at least one wheatless meal a day.

Every day, thousands scanned newspaper casualty lists for familiar names, hoping against hope they wouldn't find anyone they knew listed beneath the stark headings: "WOUNDED," "DIED OF WOUNDS," or "KILLED IN ACTION." At last, through prohibition, families could do something to support and honour their husbands, fathers and sons serving overseas. The connection between the enjoyment of a pint of brew or bottle of rye and the carnage endured in the trenches seems tenuous now, but it didn't seem that way in 1916, when it was easy—even reassuring—for sorrowing families of the dead and wounded to forge a personal link between their bereavement and the battle against booze. As he sat behind his desk, John Nelson could take pride in his role in winning the whisky war in BC—and, in doing so, winning that other war in Europe.

The saloon's days were numbered. Bowing to prohibitionist pressure, the BC government had already outlawed 19th-century free-standing bars. By 1914, bars were found only inside hotels. Not long before, saloons had been the only site of "culture," but now there were new theatres in major American and Canadian coastal cities, and the automobile made it easier for audiences to travel to see urban attractions. Many cities boasted libraries and even art galleries. Drinking establishments—and even live-entertainment venues—faced a new competitor, and by 1916, it was no passing fancy. The moving picture was here to stay.

People everywhere were talking about the new movie stars—Mary Pickford, Francis X. Bushman and racy Theda Bara. When fans weren't paying a nickel to watch them, they were paying a dime to read about them in *Motion Picture* and *Photoplay* magazines. Movies became family entertainment when moms and dads took the kiddies to see cowboy shoot-'em-ups starring Tom Mix and William S. Hart and the manic comedies of the Keystone Kops. No saloon ever enjoyed such a wide clientele.

British Columbia prohibitionists had been heartened by news from Washington communities that had gone dry through local option votes. During the 1912 state election campaign, prohibitionists had claimed "A Dry Town Is

Good for Bellingham" and published facts and figures to prove it. Since Bellingham's 43 saloons had been boarded up the year before, the four-page pamphlet stated, "The police force has been reduced fully one-third, and even then, find [*sic*] less to do than formerly." When saloons had been "running the town," there were almost a thousand drunks arrested in 1910 alone, and homicides "were of frequent occurrence." Only 169 drunks had slept it off in police cells during the first eight months of 1912, and in that period, there hadn't been one murder committed. Despite losing $48,000 in liquor revenue, Bellingham was now "in better condition financially" than before. The population was growing, bank deposits were increasing and the number of building permits had skyrocketed. Eleven saloons had done a roaring trade in Wenatchee, a town of 3,500. With the saloons gone, a former mayor reported the town had nearly doubled in size, and now boasted "more civic development in this short space of time . . . than any city in the West."

As BC voters lined up at the polls, the news was even better. In Spokane, tax collection was easier, delinquency was down 50 percent and drunk arrests were down 67 percent. The *Daily World* reported that after just six months, Spokane's prohibition enforcement "has done away with one-half to two-thirds of the poverty and crime in the city." Walla Walla's mayor announced drunkenness was down 80 percent. All this was a mixed blessing for State Highway Commissioner George F. Cotterill, however. Fewer state prison convicts meant he was forced to contract paid labourers to undertake road repairs.

When voters in smaller centres and rural areas tipped the balance and Washington State went dry, Spokane and Seattle had voted wet. However, once big-city folks experienced prohibition's initial benefits, most happily embraced prohibition, even though it cost their state the commerce of brewers, distillers and over a thousand saloons, and former employees lost their livelihoods. Some jobs went to wet San Francisco, the new location of Seattle Brewing and Malting (Rainier Beer), and its subsidiary, Independent Brewing Company. Brewers left behind were forced to make weak near-beer, sodas and other non-alcoholic drinks. Hotelmen and brewers lobbied hard for prohibition exemptions. One bill would have allowed the manufacture of beer sold directly to consumers, and another allowed the sales and consumption inside hotels. Elections in 1916 gave a solid majority the opportunity to vote no, defeating both bills.

Among the most prominent prohibition converts was the *Seattle Daily Times* editor, Major C.B. Blethen. His father's newspaper once had "fought its damnedest against Prohibition," C.B. admitted. But statistics made Blethen a believer. As he revealed proudly in widely read magazines such as *Collier's National Weekly*, money formerly poured into tumblers was flowing into savings accounts. In addition, "There was not a grocery store in Seattle that did not show an increase in business." That implied happy kids were munching regular meals. As the *Daily World*'s John Nelson put it, "DOLLARS ONCE SPENT IN BARS FILL LARDERS."

BC prohibitionists must have rejoiced. How much better life would be in a dry world! And when that great day came, on October 1, 1917, Rogers, Nelson and every prohibitionist took pride in finally convincing the province's people to follow the righteous path already taken by Alberta, Saskatchewan and Manitoba. Tucking the Women's Christian Temperance Union under its spreading wings, the PPA had transformed western Canada's wet holdout, rough and raw British Columbia, into a moral, upstanding province.

It's unlikely that BC drys read a sobering comment made by Portland's police chief in January 1916. Like most Portland residents (who had voted wet), John Clark wasn't cheered by the drys' narrow state victory. Astute lawmen realized that fewer drunks meant fewer dollars; belt-tightening would occur just as remaining patrolmen in diminished squads had an additional law to uphold.

"While prohibition has a tendency to decrease certain types of crime," Clark stated cautiously, "we now have this [prohibition] law to enforce, which requires careful attention on the part of police officers." Police chiefs were not usually noted for understatement. It would soon become obvious that Clark was an exception to the rule. Chief Clark was likely not only referring to money but, more ominously, to his men's morality.

On July 18, just weeks before BC voted on liquor's future, a small story on the back pages of both the *Vancouver Sun* and *Daily World* caught the eye of both prohibitionists and "drink men" alike. Three plainclothes members of the Seattle police Prohibition Enforcement Squad pulled up in their unmarked car near the waterfront. One of the three walked briskly across the busy street and disappeared into the bar of the Ferguson Hotel. Five minutes later, as planned, his companions, W.W. Morris and C.V. Harvey, walked through the doors. The officer leaning against the bar turned and gestured at the full glass in front of him. The bartender, J.A. Farnham, had just poured him a whisky, a clear breach of the new law. When an officer reached out to grab the bottle as evidence, another drinker at the bar, William Bothwell, leaped to Farnham's defence and ordered the trio out. The policemen reached inside their coats for badges to warn the drinker off, but instead of meekly allowing the police to arrest the bartender, Bothwell reached inside his own coat and pulled out a revolver. Morris reached out to grab Bothwell's weapon as Harvey leaped the bar to grab Farnham, who now also brandished a handgun.

Multiple gunshots split the air. Within seconds, both Morris and Harvey were hit—one in the arm, one in the leg. Bothwell slumped to the floor, bleeding from four bullet wounds, down but not out. He reached across the floor, snatching at his fallen gun. Harvey stepped up, kicked the gun away and smashed his service revolver into Bothwell's face for good measure.

Within minutes, the Ferguson was crawling with cops. Police ensured that Farnham reached city jail safely, but when Bothwell reached City Hospital, he was dead. The hospital morgue's newest arrival was no insignificant barfly. William Bothwell was a former city comptroller employed at the time of his death as a special police agent recruited to combat dockside labour unrest. That fact may explain why he was armed. Bothwell exemplified a disturbing prohibition truth: thirst made a mockery out of good-guy/bad-guy stereotypes. The next person thrown behind bars or laid out on a gurney might be someone's respected employer, friendly neighbour or beloved relative.

The *Daily World* ran the story as "GUNFIGHT AT BAR HAS FATAL ENDING." The *Vancouver Sun* printed "ATTEMPT TO ENFORCE PROHIBITION LAW RESULTS IN A TRAGEDY." In a tiny, terse *World* editorial, prohibitionist John Nelson said the *Sun*'s headline should have read, "ATTEMPT TO VIOLATE PROHIBITION LAW RESULTS IN TRAGEDY." Rather smugly, Nelson added, "Serious attempts to violate any law often do result that way." Quite so, fellow prohibitionists probably agreed.

However, one week later, an even more outrageous Seattle episode occurred, implicating a quartet of handsome young bootlegging brothers named Billingsley. The incident and its consequences offered troubling law-enforcement lessons for a province contemplating prohibition.

2

Tragedy in Seattle

TEN-YEAR-OLD SHERMAN BILLINGSLEY strode purposefully down the dusty Oklahoma country road, pulling on his loaded wagon. Passing farmers may have looked down on him from their wagon seats and wondered where the slim, determined farm boy in his bib overalls was headed. Jingling harnesses and thudding hooves masked the telltale clink of glass beneath the wagon's concealing blanket. A gift from Sherman's brother Logan, the wagon contained dozens of bottles of beer Logan himself had placed inside it. Sherman had become Anadarko's "baby bootlegger," recruited by his older siblings to sell beer at 50 cents a bottle. Sherman's destination was a wooded area near the tiny town of Anadarko, where Kiowa, Comanche, Wichita and Caddo hung out.

The only adults in Oklahoma Territory who couldn't purchase liquor were Native people. Anadarko—which later proclaimed itself "Indian Capital of the Nation"—was surrounded by reserves full of thirsty customers. Penalties for violating the federal Code of Indian Offences might have been the Billingsley boys' rationale for involving their youngest brother. Surely the police wouldn't jail a kid so young! Bootlegging was likely a financial necessity; in 1904, their father, Robert, had been forced to sell his successful Anadarko-area farm to pay legal bills incurred when Logan went on trial for murder.

Logan's amorous advances toward young Chloe Wheatley had a predictable result, and the pregnant girl's father demanded marriage. Logan laughed. A knife in each hand, Wheatley ambushed Logan and his father during a subsequent Anadarko shopping trip. Robert rushed their attacker. As the girl's father raised his knives to cut Robert down, Logan drew a snub-nosed, double-barrelled pistol— likely a derringer—and emptied it into Wheatley's chest. Found guilty of murder, Logan appealed on grounds of self-defence and won a second trial. The jury acquitted him in less than half an hour. Logan married Chloe anyway and soon was ostensibly employed in the family's new Anadarko confectionery store. By now, statehood and constitutionally mandated prohibition had arrived. The Billingsleys' bootleg business boomed.

By 1916, the four brothers—Sherman, Logan, Fred and

Ora—had left Oklahoma (and Logan's three prison terms for bootlegging and gambling-house operations) for the West Coast. The reason for relocation likely wasn't Logan's outstanding arrest warrant, but market size. Seattle was four times larger than Oklahoma City, the brothers' vice-ridden, oil-rich former bootleg centre, and almost ten times larger than Charleston, West Virginia, where they had most recently operated. State prohibition had turned Seattle into the country's biggest bootleg market.

Washington State wasn't quite the bone-dry liquor desert of faraway Oklahoma or of nearby Oregon, either, a fact that worked both for and against the bootlegging Billingsleys. Washington's dry laws contained an exception designed to pacify those who believed alcohol had medical uses beyond that of a disinfectant. For decades, patent medicines contained various forms of alcohol that produced a calming effect on users plagued by what were euphemistically called "female complaints" and "hysteria." Even desperate men wouldn't countenance drinking the stuff. Thanks to Washington's medicinal-use exemption, they didn't have to. Armed with a doctor's prescription, anyone could walk into a drugstore and get what they wanted—and it wasn't Lydia Pinkham's Vegetable Compound. What they took home, concealed in brown paper bags, were bottles of medicinal whisky. Three months into prohibition, more than 65 new Seattle drugstores opened up.

One store, the Stewart Street Pharmacy, was operated by

recent arrivals named Billingsley. A government pharmacy certificate limited the brothers' liquor purchases to one case at a time, but Logan made a simple certificate alteration and ordered up a thousand cases. Liquor the owners could not account for through medical prescriptions was charged to "leakage and spillage." As business was very brisk for the clumsy proprietors, gallons of liquor were "spilled" on a regular basis. Little brother Sherman still had lots to learn, however, and lessons came hard. One day he stupidly poured a store customer a drink. The customer was a dry-squad undercover agent. Sherman was arrested. The brothers hired flamboyant George Vanderveer as their defence lawyer. Having previously harangued juries as King County prosecutor, Vanderveer knew the legal system inside out. While defending the naive "country boy from Oklahoma," the lawyer cunningly faked tears. The jury took pity and returned a not-guilty verdict.

Washington's new liquor legislation made another exception. Individuals could import 2 quarts of hard booze or 12 quart bottles of full-strength beer about every three weeks for personal use. All it took was a county auditor's import permit. In Washington, it wasn't against the law to drink the stuff, except in public; what got you arrested was making or selling it. This was definitely not good news for bootleggers, which may have been the law's intent.

Eight months into prohibition, the King County auditor's office had sold 18,000 permits. The following year,

34,000 permits were purchased in Spokane County, which claimed just 33,000 registered voters. Entrepreneurs in wet states and Canadian provinces eagerly met Washington's demand; newspapers began running ads for mail-order liquor, much of it legitimate high-quality product. All a thirsty customer had to do was make a telephone call to the local number listed in an ad, place an order and, later, walk into an express office to pick it up. Adept buyers always had refreshments in the kitchen cupboard.

Major liquor "entrepreneurs" vied for bigger pieces of Seattle's bootleg pie. Foremost among them was former Seattle police officer Edward J. "Jack" Marquett. During the pre-prohibition turmoil, crooked police chief Charles (Wappy) Wappenstein had assigned Detective Marquett as the bodyguard of *Seattle Daily Times* founding publisher Colonel Alden Blethen, who championed the corrupt mayor and a money-making "open town." As fervent prohibitionists and other reformers threatened those on the sinful side of the city known as "Wappyville," Blethen feared for his safety. He should have feared for his freedom instead.

Marquett couldn't protect the newspaperman from being indicted on corruption charges. The publisher escaped jail; the police chief didn't. When prohibition came in, probably few of the (soberly) celebrating prohibitionists noticed that Detective Marquett had handed in his badge and put on a snappy three-piece suit. Marquett's objective was to make the city's entire bootleg pie his own. He didn't hesitate to eliminate upstart competitors, especially upstart newcomers such as the Billingsleys.

Major bootleggers faced serious challenges getting booze to Seattle. To the south, Oregon was dry. To the east, Idaho was dry, and Montana, like BC to the north, was about to go dry. At a time when an auto's top speed was about 20 miles per hour, hauling booze meant a very long road trip, unless the rum-runner operated near the Oregon border with wet California. Moreover, the primitive state of roads made automobile travel a nail-biting adventure. When federal and state laws made liquor importation illegal, long-distance haulers faced dry-squad roadblocks. Floating liquor up the coast from California came with different hazards—wind, weather, mechanical breakdown and 20th-century pirates called hijackers, who roared out of coves and inlets and relieved boat crews of their booze at gunpoint. One band of hijackers was led by none other than Jack Marquett. By stealing liquor, pirate Jack avoided the cost of shipping while robbing competitors of their lucrative pieces of bootleg pie. By the summer of 1916, Marquett was close to crowning himself king of Seattle bootlegging.

The Billingsleys didn't stoop to piracy to solve their shipping dilemma. These major retailers diversified and became manufacturers. Beneath an inconspicuous trap door inside their Westlake Avenue warehouse, the brothers set up a small basement operation complete with barrels of alcohol and a gallon of burnt sugar for "whisky" colouring.

The Billingsleys were still like other small-time, fly-by-night bootleggers operating makeshift stills, but Marquett must have feared the worst. How long would it be before gallons of Billingsley whisky went from vats to barrels and from barrels to bottles? With a ramp replacing the trap door, cloth-capped warehouse labourers might soon be wheeling whole cases of bottles to ground-floor storage.

With a warehouse stocked with valuable liquid inventory and facing ruthless competitors, the brothers were probably all carrying guns. However, business owners didn't personally guard their property after dark. The Billingsleys hired a night watchman at $3.50 a day, paying in cash—no forms, no contract, no records. Logan gave the new watchman a gun, too. If there was trouble, Logan told him, use it. The man who accepted the position—and the revolver—was Ichibe Suehiro, an Asian immigrant. To most people of the era, including many in polite society, Suehiro was merely an "oriental," or a "chink." The former term was more accurate than the latter; Suehiro wasn't Chinese, he was Japanese. At the time, few Americans differentiated between the two, but the law did.

Chinese immigrants were outlawed in the US. Many Washington State residents, like their BC counterparts, were convinced "those people" were bad for the country and bad for business, stealing jobs that white men, including first- or second-generation German and Irish, deserved. If an overzealous cop stopped him, Suehiro was ready; he carried papers confirming his Japanese birth. At the moment, the "chink-lovin'" Wobblies (Industrial Workers of the World) were battling the American Federation of Labour's all-white membership for work on the docks. Suehiro was lucky to have a job, yet he was far from humble.

Suehiro, or Pete, as the brothers called him, was an "odd Japanese," Sherman Billingsley later laughingly told the *Daily Times*, "always bragging about what he could and would do if he was in our shoes." Suehiro's behaviour was so cockeyed that the Billingsleys didn't take offence but merely "looked on him as a sort of comedian." After one particular July night in 1916, the brothers weren't laughing anymore.

The chaotic waterfront labour strife had resulted in potentially dangerous 12-hour shifts for Seattle's finest, which included a tall, moustachioed, 22-year police veteran, Sergeant John F. Weedin. Perched on an open platform, Weedin and his partner, police chauffeur Robert Wiley, drove a mechanized box on wheels called a Black Mariah, a genteel term substituted for "Paddy Wagon," a name coined decades before when New York cops routinely apprehended brawling Irish immigrants, or "paddies." Weedin's Mariah also doubled as the city's only ambulance.

On the night of Monday, July 24, Weedin and Wiley were shot and killed at the bootleggers' Westlake Avenue warehouse-distillery. No one seemed to know how or why. The only detail everyone agreed on was "who." The Billingsleys' night watchman was the killer. News of the shooting stunned Seattle's police force, city hall and residents. Although nine policemen had been killed in the line of duty in the force's 35-year history, never had two of their own been killed in the same incident, and likely never before in such suspicious circumstances.

The official police version of events cast the two policemen as good cops. Police maintained that teetotaller Weedin and his partner Wiley, both family men, were driving the chief's car from a downtown rooming-house squad party. With them were the boarding-house operator and her two friends. The women needed a ride, and the men gallantly offered one. They never reached the women's destination. Two strangers frantically flagged down the borrowed car and gasped out that they had been fired upon by an oriental at a nearby warehouse. The two off-duty officers investigated. Suehiro fired first on Wiley, hitting him in the groin. Wiley wasn't in uniform, but he was carrying his revolver. As he fell, he yanked it out and fatally shot Suehiro in the stomach. Suehiro's wound didn't immediately slow him down, however. He stumbled up to the car and blasted Weedin point-blank in the face, killing him instantly.

Minutes later, police found Logan Billingsley—who likely had been inside the warehouse—standing amidst the carnage. The dying men were loaded inside the Black Mariah that Weedin and Wiley had once driven and taken to hospital. Both Suehiro and Wiley gave bedside statements; Wiley even managed to phone his police buddies. The three women, who had fled the car when the shooting started, were questioned by police and charged with being accessories to murder. At a hearing, the women's testimony supported Wiley's version of the horrific episode. They were set free. The two men who allegedly stopped the cops' car were never found nor identified.

The officers' revolvers had, strangely, disappeared. Weedin was killed as he sat in the car. Why had he not jumped out to assist Wiley as gunfire broke out? Who was the "white man" a witness saw shooting at Wiley along with Suehiro and who then supposedly fled the scene? Why had the chief loaned his official car to off-duty cops? Did police coach the women before they testified? Were Wiley's statements accurate? Had the dying man even made them? Perhaps the biggest mystery was the identity of the men who had supposedly flagged down the car. Metal files and a pry bar found at the scene indicated they were break-and-enter artists. But did they even exist? Had police simply planted the tools? These unanswered questions led to suspicion, and suspicion fuelled speculation. What if . . . ?

In a bad-cop scenario, the ladies' destination could have been another party, and the two policemen might have stopped off to buy or boost some booze. Quite reasonably, the two cops would have shrugged off the consequences of relieving the bootleggers of a few bottles—or even an entire case—of liquor. Storing illegal booze, the brothers were hardly in a position to complain. If they were stupid enough to report the theft, they would risk being arrested.

The Billingsleys would regard the loss as a cost of doing business and merely change their locks.

Assuming the cops knew the whereabouts of the warehouse and what it contained, they probably didn't know about boastful watchman Ichibe Suehiro. Leaving Weedin behind the wheel, Wiley could have walked to the rear of the warehouse either to buy liquor or break in. To the man hired to safeguard the warehouse, a furtive figure at the door certainly would have looked like—to use Logan's word—trouble. Finding himself unexpectedly in the Billingsleys' shoes, Suehiro made good on his boasts and began shooting.

The specific circumstances of the fatal shootout are still open to conjecture; however, what happened next is not. Police immediately arrested three Billingsley brothers and their father. Sherman, who had eloped with an Oklahoma girl, escaped immediate arrest. By the time the front-page newspaper story hit the streets, all were free on bail. Charged with first-degree murder, Logan escaped to San Francisco. Watching from the sidelines was Jack Marquett. Pirate Jack likely concluded the murder charge against Logan wouldn't stick; Suehiro's confession was backed up by the bullets recovered during Weedin's autopsy and Wiley's surgery. In the backlash of the killings, Marquett must have also wondered when police would come to arrest him as well. He began to strategize how he might avoid arrest and, at the same time, rid his syndicate of major competitors.

3

The Trouble with
City Hall

WHEN SEATTLE RESIDENTS NEEDED tangible evidence of city-hall corruption, all they had to do was look over at the building later known to two generations as the Lester Apartments. The sprawling two- and three-storey, flat-roofed wooden structure on Tenth Avenue South wasn't originally constructed as an apartment block. In 1910, the Lester had been designed and built as an enormous brothel, housing close to 500 prostitutes in rows of 8-by-12-foot rooms. The two so-called vice lords who spearheaded the audacious project needed friends in high places to pull it off and knew where to find them: inside the new beaux arts–styled Seattle Public Safety Building at 400 Yesler Way.

The developers sought out Seattle mayor Hiram Gill

and his police chief, Charles Wappenstein. Prostitution had enriched them both. Lawyer Gill had specialized in defending underworld types not unlike the men behind the project. Wappenstein had lined his pockets with direct payoffs from local madams and pimps. Gill asked city council to duly consider the development proposal. The council did so and quickly passed an ordinance giving the Hillside Improvement Company a 15-year lease on the street.

The men behind the Hillside Improvement Company didn't have to put up their own money for the project. Stock was offered openly. Given the seemingly insatiable market for the business to be conducted on the site and the open-town tolerance of the era, Hillside appeared to be a low-risk proposition. Shares were eagerly snapped up.

As blatant as all this was, it took undercover detectives hired by "the Black-Maned Lion," charismatic Presbyterian prohibitionist Reverend Mark Matthews, to bring Gill down and send police chief Wappy to prison. The taint from the corruption investigation—not to mention the brothel itself—sent Seattle voters back to the mayoralty ballot box prematurely, on February 7, 1911. Through a rare mid-term recall vote, Seattle residents of both sexes (women had won the vote just three months before) tossed Gill out of city hall. Gill ran for office again the very next year, lost, and returned to his law practice. The Hillside Improvement Building was completed as the Lester Apartments and became home for working-class renters.

Hiram Gill was an inveterate opportunist who well understood which way the political winds were blowing. If supporting the lawless couldn't get him elected to city hall, he would get elected by supporting the lawful. All he had to do was change his open-town principles to closed-town principles. Changing principles was easy for Hi Gill.

During the 1914 election, Gill deftly capitalized on reform's rapidly growing appeal, capturing votes by stridently vowing to break the back of the city's liquor, gambling and prostitution interests. The strategy won Gill a four-year term.

Beginning on January 1, 1916, the very first day of the state's dry era, city hall embarked on a series of attacks against lawbreakers and did so with a vehemence that would have been unthinkable in BC. In one of the greatest ironies in West Coast prohibition history, the man who led the charge against liquor lawbreakers had previously been thrown out of city hall—and almost thrown into jail—for his link to crimes he now vowed to stamp out.

Quite literally, the axe came down. The police department dry squad went to work inside the American Cafe. The room-length mirror exploded in a geyser of glass shards. Large light fixtures were severed from their cords and driven against the walls, falling to the floor in tangles of metal. Tables were hacked to pieces and chairs smashed and strewn over floors awash in spilled liquor. Sweating men levered themselves atop the bar and swung their axes, splintering and gouging. Before it was over, this riot

30

of destruction and ones like it undertaken in Portland by "sledgehammer squads" had reduced scores of prohibition-defying drinking spots to wreckage.

No one accused Hiram Gill of reneging on his campaign promises. Instead, some citizens began complaining of the destruction wrought by them. Two raids alone resulted in over $200,000 in damages. It didn't help that Gill's punitive actions extended to some of the city's best-known citizens. The homes of aircraft manufacturer William Boeing, shipbuilder David E. Skinner and other members of Seattle's elite were raided. It didn't seem to matter that the confiscated liquor was legally held in cellars or kitchen; its possibly illegal purchase was enough to initiate police action. The physical damage to opulent homes was slight, but the damage to their owners' reputations was more serious. Ironically, through his efforts Gill was making enemies among the lawful.

By 1917, Washington state prohibition had become even more deeply entrenched. In a move that Spokane's *Spokesman-Review* warned "would be more likely to stimulate bootlegging than to diminish it," the state joined Oregon in becoming "bone dry," outlawing all manner of liquor importation. That meant importers Jack Marquett, the Billingsleys and others were now engaged in another illegal activity. Little wonder the Billingsleys were diversifying into manufacturing, while Marquett wondered how long it would be before he was languishing inside a jail cell on the Public Safety Building's top floor.

Seattle mayor Hiram Gill was thrown out of office but re-elected in 1914 after promising to crack down on liquor violators. He was soon indicted as a violator himself.

SEATTLE MUNICIPAL ARCHIVES 12278

For an alleged promise of immunity, Marquett persuaded Hunt Liquor Company, San Francisco liquor wholesalers, to turn over business correspondence linking the Billingsleys to illegal liquor importation. Meanwhile, Vanderveer was making his own deal with County Prosecutor Alfred Lundin: drop the murder charge in exchange for a guilty plea on conspiracy to violate liquor laws. Lundin—who had served as deputy prosecutor under Vanderveer—had been hounding the Billingsleys relentlessly. Lundin agreed. During the Billingsleys' trial, the defence dropped a bombshell.

Logan testified that a month after the off-duty cops had been killed, he had withdrawn $4,000 from his hotel safety-deposit box, carried it to city hall and handed it directly to Mayor Hiram Gill. The four grand was the price for the return of the brothers' whisky-business records seized by police. Logan walked into Gill's office with his cash and walked out with his files. On the stand, Logan admitted this wasn't the first time he had paid to protect his business and himself. Other palms greased belonged to the sheriff, the police chief and four officers. The agreed amount was $10 for each barrel of whisky in the warehouse. Many realized that the Billingsleys were still playing the payoff game; Vanderveer had walked into the district attorney's office with inside information and had walked out with a promise of leniency. The mayor, the former police chief and the four policemen were all indicted. The four-week trial riveted the public.

Guilty pleas on liquor charges netted Ora just 30 days in the jug; Fred got 6 months and Logan was sentenced to 13 months. Logan's appeal process gained him some additional freedom, but he finally entered McNeil Island prison in May 1918. While Hi Gill avoided jail, Jack Marquett did not. As the *Port Townsend Leader* put it, "Prior arrangements concerning immunity were entirely ignored, Margett [*sic*], the originator of the proceedings . . . getting the same dose which was handed to the others."

Once released, Sherman, Ora and Fred Billingsley moved to Detroit and began doing what came naturally: bootlegging and rum-running. After Fred helped him break out of prison, Logan was back east, too, running five-dollar cases of Canadian Club from Windsor, Ontario, and selling them in the Motor City for $150 each. At the height of US Prohibition, Sherman opened a New York speakeasy called the Stork Club, a high-class nightspot that attracted the rich and famous for another 40 years.

Hiram Gill managed to finish his term in office this time around, but even before it ended, there were demands for another recall. Businessmen were angered by the city's sullied reputation. The public was mortified at Gill's stained personal image (to add to the Billingsley indictment, Gill had also been disbarred for a year on an ethics charge). City-hall axe raids had been effective prohibition show-biz, but despite the costly damage they inflicted, liquor-related graft and corruption were thriving, as courtroom revelations made by Logan and Fred Billingsley demonstrated so dramatically.

The Ferguson Hotel shootout and Billingsley warehouse triple slaying carried a very serious implication. Prohibition wasn't preventing lawlessness, it was creating it. Nevertheless, these episodes likely only reinforced BC residents' opinions about stateside corruption and violence. Conditions and people were different in BC, so prohibition would be different there, too. Dry advocates were sure of it.

4

Law and Disorder

UP THE WINDING GRAVEL ROAD east of Hope, BC, at Princeton's BC Provincial Police (BCPP) station, Chief Constable J.A. Fraser had a problem. It wasn't a typical law-enforcement issue. Fraser wouldn't have bothered writing Superintendent William G. McMynn about that. Fraser and his men knew how to deal with a brawler, a suspected thief or a murderer. While it might be another year or so before details of the Prohibition Act made it into the officers' manuals, he and his men knew the basics; there certainly had been enough circulars and directives about it.

For example, if they caught the local hotel operator serving full-strength beer, officers knew what action to take. In the unlikely event (given the size of their territory) that they stumbled upon low-lifes slaving over a liquor still, officers simply informed the federal inspector. Manufacturing was a federal offence, not a provincial one. But there were no rules for the bizarre situation Fraser now faced.

Prohibition or not, Fraser's men were still collaring drunks. When they did a routine check on the jailed inebriates, the chief constable wrote, officers found them "all dead to the world this morning." Throughout the night, the prisoners had managed to sample liquor from confiscated kegs stored in the next cell. The kegs had been "a source of trouble ever since they were seized," the frustrated Fraser told McMynn. "The sooner we get rid of the infernal stuff the better pleased I will be." Because the law didn't cover this situation, the likely solution for disposing of "the infernal stuff" was to dump it out back. Some suspicious residents may have deduced that instead of dumping the booze, off-duty officers were knocking it back at a party somewhere. Many would have not thought the worse of them for doing so.

As BC residents were soon to discover, there were more serious prohibition predicaments than tippling prison-cell drunks. Not all issues plaguing the province's people and policemen were the result of prohibition; some came about because of what prohibition still allowed.

Despite prohibition, BC residents could still buy liquor. The easiest way to do that, as in Washington State, was to see a doctor. A medical prescription allowed a patient to buy liquor from a druggist or one of the government liquor stores operated for this specific purpose. Although the government's price list of medicinal-relief liquors warned purchasers that "the sale of liquor as a beverage is prohibited," the list included some surprising remedies, including champagne, gin and five-gallon jars of beer.

It became apparent that the instrument most often used by GPs in patient treatment—alongside stethoscopes and tongue depressors—was the Waterman fountain pen. By April 1919, BC physicians had written an estimated 300,000 prescriptions for medicinal liquor. BC's entire post-war population was about 450,000. Even taking into account return patients, 300,000 prescriptions meant a huge proportion of BC's population was running to the doctor to get a drink. When the average worker earned four dollars a day, even the lowest-cost prescription fee represented a half-day's pay. Little wonder some doctors were writing as many as 4,000 prescriptions a month. For many, prohibition represented a windfall.

Like Chief Constable J.A. Fraser, a frustrated executive secretary decided to write a letter to his own boss, BC's premier. Vancouver people were standing in queues a quarter of a mile long to fill prescriptions at government liquor stores, Harlan Brewster's secretary reported. "Hindus, Chinese, Japanese . . . a kaleidoscopic procession waiting in the rain for a replenishment that would drive the chills away, and it was alleged that several doctors needed a little alcoholic liniment to soothe the writer's cramp caused by inditing their signatures at two dollars per line."

But thirsty people didn't need to step furtively into a drugstore clutching a liquor prescription, nor hobnob with the multitude shuffling along in a liquor-store queue. Like Washington State residents, BC imbibers could simply receive their bottles by relatively discreet out-of-province mail order, at least until federal import laws changed.

People had been convinced to vote for prohibition, in part, because doing so would outlaw bars. However, on the very first dry day, 60 of Vancouver's 69 hotel bars opened as usual. Regular beer contained 10 percent proof spirits, or about 5.7 percent alcohol by volume. Bartenders now poured legal "near-beer" brew containing less than 2.5 percent proof spirits. Initially, this happy fact had hotel owners smiling. However, since near-beer was not considered liquor, there was no restriction on who could sell it. Unlicensed bars opened up everywhere. Hotel operators were soon screaming "unfair competition." Because it wasn't liquor, there was no age restriction on the weak brew, either. "There is nothing [in law] to prevent even the youngest boys and girls from purchasing and drinking near beer," Attorney General John W. Farris admitted.

What prohibition had undeniably achieved was to put hundreds of people out of work. Bars, not rooms, kept most hotels profitable, so many hotels closed. The province's sole distillery was shuttered. By prohibition's final year, only 13 of the 31 breweries operating in 1910 had survived by supplying near-beer for local and regional markets and, in a few cases, by exporting full-strength suds to whatever wet American states they could ship to. Sometimes a truck carrying export beer made a clandestine delivery to a BC bar. If caught, operators faced a serious offering-for-sale charge punishable by 6 to 12 months of hard labour. However, many jurists considered this sentence overly harsh. It was much simpler, faster—and more compassionate—for the operator to plead to the relatively minor charge of "possession not in a private dwelling" to expedite a quick fine payment. The PPA executive secretary, Reverend W.G. Fortune, called such courtroom leniency "trifling with justice."

Few hotel-bar operators were charged for selling whisky or full-strength beer. In smaller communities, these individuals were friends and neighbours. So were local BCPP officers. Sometimes the bonds of friendship and community superceded the spirit of cooperation between law-enforcement agencies. "When a Mountie was coming to town he had to notify the city [BCPP] policeman," a former bartender at Cumberland's King George Hotel recalled many decades later. "So as soon as the city policeman got to hear that the Mounties were coming, he'd phone the hotel and say, 'Don't sell anything today.'"

"I think Prohibition caused more problems than it cured," reflected another former BCPP officer. When operators of "second-class joints" said that they were turning a profit on near-beer, he remained skeptical. "I recall finding a large supply of liquors behind a removable panel on a soft-drink bar. The senior constable and me poured it all out and told the owner that if he tried to replace it, [the senior constable] would have to charge him next time."

"I didn't know anybody, teetotaller . . . or drinker, who thought Prohibition legislation was beneficial or enforceable," a former BCPP policeman wrote to Lynne Stonier-Newman, author of the force's definitive history. "Most [people] were sympathetic to the small hotel owners who were being forced out of business." On the eve of prohibition, hoteliers also faced the matter of liquor inventories. "Some supervision of how the liquor was disposed of was cursory," the former BCPP policeman admitted, "particularly since the government was so slow about making [inventory compensation] payments to the poor blokes. Quantities of wines and liquors were listed as 'given away,' on the licensee claim forms but most of that was probably used to stock private cellars at cost."

Understaffed, overworked and burdened with a law they couldn't effectively enforce, BCPP officers appeared to be doing their best. "The men are conscientious, with good integrity," Superintendent McMynn reported to Attorney General Farris at the end of 1920. McMynn added that the force dismissed only one man the previous year. The policeman in question was cashiered not for theft, nor on a morals charge, but for drinking. No doubt he wasn't the only BCPP officer who imbibed; others were likely more careful in choosing a time and place to tilt a glass or tip a bottle.

In BC, Washington and Oregon, the number of drunks arrested fell markedly. In the first eight and a half months of 1915, Portland police threw 6,495 drunks into the tank. In the same period the following year—the first eight months of state prohibition—the number was just 1,802, a stunning decrease of 72.3 percent. Portland's plummeting arrest rate wasn't the result of the bad guys leaving town (although "more are going all the time," a Portland police lieutenant claimed) nor a sudden embracing of temperance. People complained of lackadaisical law enforcement.

In reply to a letter about enforcement concerns from well-known Congregationalist Reverend A.E. Cooke, John Farris confessed, "The real problem [of enforcement] was the lack of enthusiasm . . . the Vancouver police have as many or more men than we [the provincial government's BCPP] have in the whole province, and if Vancouver cannot police itself, it is time people looked the situation fairly in the face." It is unclear what "situation" the Attorney General was referring to—police failings or prohibition itself. By 1920, Farris's disgust with the latter was no secret. The previous fall, the Attorney General had told the Nelson chapter of the Women's Christian Temperance Union that if liquor legislation wasn't revised soon, he would resign. Yet when he was finally forced to resign, it was for a far different reason.

If police spent more time busting bootleg operations than hauling in drunks, it wasn't just because manufacturing and selling liquor contravened the Prohibition Act on its most basic level. Bootleggers' successes raised howls of protest from hotel owners, whose legal near-beer bars found it difficult to compete. It was a good argument, and for some, a good cover. Many hotel-bar operators were bootleggers' preferred customers. They poured the illegal product into easy-to-empty pitchers in case they received a tip that an inspector was about to drop by.

The higher a bootlegger's sales figures rose, the tougher it got for him to keep his operation a secret. The PPA claimed that the Vancouver dry squad had seized at least 121 bootleg stills by March 1920. The previous year, squad members had knelt inside a bedroom closet and crawled through a trap door to reach an 80-gallon still in the attic of one home. The floor had been reinforced to take the extra weight of the still and its product, and zinc sheeting had been installed to prevent leaks. There were certainly enough bootleggers to keep police busy—but at a higher cost than the province or any of its towns could afford. For that reason alone, prohibition enforcement was often a hit-and-miss affair.

Once prohibition was law, BC residents might have expected the PPA to disband, its mandate successfully fulfilled. However, the PPA convinced the government that it had a life in the dry world as a prohibition watchdog. Through the new Prohibition Act, the association was given the right to appoint a prohibition commissioner to oversee the importation and storage of liquor distributed to doctors, pharmacies, veterinarians and religious organizations that used wine in their rituals. In 1919, the PPA's Reverend Fortune complained to his newly appointed liquor commissioner, Colonel J. Sclater, that the law was being flaunted openly in the Vancouver Island town of Alberni. The commissioner replied that he was not surprised that "drunkeness [*sic*] is rife in Alberni" and added, "Drunkeness is, I am sorry to say, not confined to Alberni and so long as the present Act remains in effect I do not see how drunkeness is to be prevented."

The PPA executive secretary knew the commissioner had no power of search, seizure or arrest. All Sclater could do was report the problem to local police. Fortune must have concluded that directing complaints to the commissioner was largely a waste of time. Perhaps he also despaired about the personal attitude of the commissioner himself. Sclater's words implied passive acceptance of the situation. But that was not Fortune's—nor the PPA's—style.

The prohibition watchdog decided its bark was not enough. What it needed was the "bite" of criminal investigation. The PPA hired private detectives. Citizens were encouraged to become stool pigeons, forwarding their own findings to the PPA. At least one concerned citizen felt obliged to give Fortune some tips for hiring men who were politely referred to as "operatives." A snitch needed good cover; "a lumber jack looking over the country or a travelling agent or teacher," the writer suggested, and he should be someone who was "a good mixer" and could mingle easily "with the worst classes." Obviously ignorant about small-town social strata (lofty-thinking school teachers seldom mixed "with the worse classes"), the writer was on firmer ground when he claimed,"The whisky ring have [sic] a spy on you, for each time you send a detective up here he is announced before he arrives."

A friendly Penticton prohibitionist wrote to inform Fortune that a "carload" of 600 cases of whisky had arrived in town and been secreted away in a known private cellar in preparation for resale. The writer wondered "if this is not a good opportunity to have a private detective sent here, for most of us have no confidence in the chief of police." In the end, the PPA's bite wasn't much more effective than its bark, simply because the watchdog lacked the teeth of official law-enforcement agencies. Police didn't always bare their teeth in their pursuit of liquor outlaws, either. No one knows how much actual corruption—kickbacks or direct sales activity—existed within the ranks of city blue or BCPP khaki. Records of suspensions, disciplinary actions and reports on rank-and-file liquor offences disappeared decades ago. When the RCMP assumed BCPP duties in 1950, it cleaned house. To the chagrin of modern historians, the discarded material likely included investigative records about what became the biggest law-enforcement and political scandal of BC's prohibition era.

5

Betrayal and Backlash

IT IS EASY TO IMAGINE the euphoria of PPA membership after its dry victory at the polls. The new Prohibition Act itself validated the organization by allowing it to choose the province's prohibition commissioner. Not surprisingly, the first commissioner the prohibition watchdog appointed was one of its own members.

Walter Chester Findlay was a hard-working individual of seemingly sterling moral character. One of the association's initial organizers, Findlay had worked closely with members of the PPA's inner circle. Moreover, during the liquor wars, Findlay never hesitated to roll up his sleeves and go to work "in the trenches." During the enormously successful 1915 Vancouver Temperance Convention, many saw how efficiently Findlay organized and supervised a staff of 75 ushers to seat 4,000 attendees. Findlay made no speeches and slapped no backs; he just cheerfully followed orders and got the job done.

Obviously, someone who had demonstrated such commitment and shouldered his responsibilities so ably deserved to be rewarded. The decision-makers probably never considered Findlay's appointment as patronage—let alone uttered the term—although that is what it clearly resembled. Outwardly, Findlay appeared honoured by his appointment; inwardly, the satisfaction he felt was due to the almost unlimited opportunities the position presented for personal gain.

In early December 1918, just over a year after the commissioner had landed the job, he was out of it. Newspaper reporters learned something was up when a government order-in-council bounced Findlay out on his ear. Then they discovered there was a warrant out for his arrest. Events had unfolded swiftly. The day after he lost his job, Findlay was turned back by police in Blaine, Washington. Minutes later, BCPP officers stopped him near the border. He remained in custody for a day—not inside a cold, barred cell but in a comfortable room in BCPP Vancouver headquarters—before posting $2,000 bail.

Findlay was free, but the charge of illegal importation of alcohol remained. Not surprisingly, no liquor had been confiscated when he was taken into custody. Findlay was merely "on the lam," as 25-cent pulp magazines put it, a fugitive fleeing arrest. The public learned that the charge of importation meant much more than stashing a case of booze or a burlap sack full of bottles in a car trunk. The now-former commissioner was accused of importing a boxcar of the stuff: 700 cases (about 8,400 bottles) of rye whisky. This wasn't hooch dripped from the tube on an attic still, either. The name on the label of each sealed bottle—Gooderham and Worts—must have raised eyebrows. The esteemed 19th-century Ontario distillery, once promoted as the biggest in the world, had been producing expensive drinking pleasures for close to a century. At the time, the street price of a single bottle of G&W cost an office steno or retail clerk about two-and-a-half-days' wages. This particular rye was destined not for pharmacies and liquor stores, but instead for Walter the rum-runner's bootleg contacts, who likely included operators of high-end hotel bars, and affluent residents who carried bottles or cases home to some of the city's toniest neighbourhoods.

Ironically, Findlay was exposed by the PPA's preferred method of ferreting out criminals: the snitch. Nelson and Fortune would have laughed if someone had told them that one of their own would be fingered by the same method, but that is what happened. Someone within the commissioner's office or close to it may have been offended by what he had seen or overheard, or wondered about large amounts of liquor mysteriously moving in and out of four different government warehouses. Or perhaps someone simply figured the law might pay for information he had stumbled across.

Frustrated authorities never found the paper trail needed to convict Findlay and his presumed cohorts for significant liquor violations. Ironically, it might have been the lack of purchase, sales and delivery paperwork that aroused the snitch's suspicion. At the time, only a handful of people knew the identity of the snitch and the evidence he offered; only a few more knew the inner workings of the PPA's very own rum-running operation. Eventually, lawmen and bootleggers took much of what they knew to their graves.

PPA members were predictably shocked at Findlay's arrest. Shock turned to outrage when Findlay pleaded guilty. (Police might have been surprised, too. A quick confession may have been Findlay's attempt to halt further investigation.) There was no jail sentence imposed, simply a fine of $1,000, a tiny fraction of what the contraband booze was worth on the market and an amount Findlay likely paid with ease. Then he left for Seattle, his intended destination when he had been initially apprehended.

The despairing PPA president, John Nelson, had asked Findlay for an explanation. Findlay gave Nelson nothing. The wrath of the PPA was expressed formally in a unanimous resolution in which Findlay's other crimes were stated as "gross fraud and breach of trust." Findlay was also guilty of making a fool out of BC Attorney General John Farris, who at one point claimed that Findlay was a "capable official," in whom Farris had the "the utmost confidence." Given that the PPA had distanced itself from Findlay, it would have been easy—and appropriate, given Findlay's confession—for Farris to do the same. Why didn't he?

The government opposition leader pounced. Former Liberal premier Billy Bowser claimed that "the Attorney-General had knowledge of his [Findlay's] rascality." Moreover, Farris had quashed Findlay's arrest warrant and warned police to leave him be. "Wasn't it strange," the leader of the opposition mused, "that Findlay's counsel had been a close political friend of the Attorney General?" Bowser then concluded what many others had suspected all along. One type of justice was meted out to the man who sold a bottle, quite another type for someone who sold enough booze to fill a boxcar.

The Attorney General's ill-advised support of Findlay finally sealed his political fate. Farris was forced to resign from cabinet in 1922. Incredible as it seems, the province's top cop had, to some degree, taken the fall for a rum-runner.

When forced to appear at a Royal Commission on illegal importation organized just two weeks after his arrest, Findlay proved uncooperative. Unlike bootlegger Billingsley, Walter the rum-runner didn't seek out a deal with the authorities. Instead, they offered him one—immunity on a theft charge and leniency with respect to other charges. But to seal the deal, Findlay had to talk. Also unlike Billingsley, Findlay never did so—not to the

Royal Commission, the PPA, nor to the new premier, John Oliver. "He absolutely refused to tell me a thing," the premier reported, other than "he had brought the liquor in as charged." So, in spite of the Attorney General's efforts to keep him out of jail, that is where Findlay eventually went. Convicted of breach of trust and abuse of position, he was sentenced to two years behind bars.

However, Findlay never breached the trust with the people who really mattered to him—whoever they were. "Big Fish" Findlay appeared important enough to gain the support of the Attorney General and be called to account by none other than the premier himself. When pressured, big fish often sacrifice the minnows swimming beneath them. Yet Findlay's silence may have protected loyal, hard-working men in his employ; there was no hint Findlay fingered lesser men. But perhaps the former liquor commissioner was, in fact, working for others, too. Many suspected the bootlegging involved individuals above Findlay. Had Findlay's silence enabled those bigger fish to swim away undetected in that sea of liquor? Was Findlay's silence purchased? If so, at what price? And who paid it? The mysteries linger, unsolved.

The Findlay affair battered prohibitionists already bruised by legal loopholes, the increased bootlegging activity and lacklustre policing. In the spring of 1919, the PPA took it on the chin again. In North Vancouver, a Methodist anniversary promised to be a swell affair. Enjoying a prominent position on the church's invitation list was long-standing PPA executive M.B. Martinson, now the association's main man on the north shore and also, significantly, the city's police commissioner. Ironically, it was high-profile Martinson's strident criticism of law enforcement gone soft on liquor that would cause his humiliating fall from grace.

During the anniversary celebration, Martinson was approached by North Vancouver mayor G.W. Vance and a police officer. The men asked Martinson to accompany them back to his home, where a search would be undertaken. Police seemed very confident that if they just kept looking, they would discover what they had come to find. Policemen even shovelled through the coal bin located beneath the kitchen. There, buried under the black lumps of fuel, officers discovered a jar of whisky.

Possession of liquor obtained legally through a doctor's prescription and enjoyed within a private residence—regardless of where it was kept—was not a crime. However, Martinson ran his professional office out of his home. Therefore, his residence was, in the strict legal sense, also a commercial enterprise. The liquor discovery meant Martinson was guilty of "possession not in a private dwelling." Outraged, Martinson protested that the whisky had been planted and that he hadn't taken a drink in 18 years.

The informant who inspired the search, seizure and charge brought against the staunch, religious prohibitionist was Arthur Davies. Zealot Martinson's law-enforcement criticisms had cost Davies his job as North Vancouver's police chief. Davies came into possession of evidence documenting liquor deliveries made to Martinson's "commercial" address and gave it to the Crown. The Crown produced it in court, and Martinson was found guilty. He appealed. A sympathetic judge overturned the verdict and Martinson was released. However, the damage had been done.

For the average person, having a charge of liquor possession overturned would amount to vindication and cause for a modest celebration, probably in the usual fashion. However, legal innocence is not the same as moral innocence. The appeal victory could offer no vindication in the eyes of Martinson's peers. It is not known what action the PPA took against its North Vancouver leader, but it is probable that Martinson was quietly relieved of his PPA position and formally cast out from the association and more informally from the members' social circle. If so, Martinson would have suffered lifelong social stigma that would have been as punishing as a lengthy stretch behind bars.

Thus, for many people, the term "prohibitionist" became synonymous with "hypocrite." How many others— good people all—could have been labelled the same, but through luck or stealth simply escaped legal penalties and the attention of the press? For this reason and others, the word "repeal" was on many lips, including those belonging to a group of powerful business leaders intent on casting out BC's Prohibition Act itself.

CHAPTER

6

The End and the Beginning

Four and twenty Yankees, feeling very dry,
Went across the border to get a drink of rye.
When the rye was opened, the Yanks began to sing,
"God bless America, but God save the King!"

—HEARD BY EDWARD, PRINCE OF WALES,

DURING HIS 1919 TOUR OF CANADA

IN FEBRUARY 1920, A CONTINGENT of 50 concerned PPA members climbed the gangway of a Canadian Pacific *Princess* steamer in Vancouver. The group was on a rescue mission to save prohibition. In the province's capital, the delegation petitioned Premier John Oliver to reorganize prohibition enforcement. The PPA had decided the how-to details could not be left to Oliver's inept government.

The PPA had a plan. All it wanted now was the government's endorsement.

The PPA planned to terminate all government prohibition administrators and replace them with a triumvirate of commissioners. The new commissioners would take their orders not from Cabinet but from a board of "outstanding citizens at large"—likely key PPA administrators. The association proposed to wrest prohibition enforcement away from the provincial government and put it into the hands of "the people."

The Attorney General had some strong feelings about this jaw-dropping proposal. While he might happily "shoulder the responsibility off on someone else," John Farris said, neither he nor the government would sanction the concept. The plan went far beyond being merely un-British; it was positively undemocratic. Happily for Farris and Oliver, another equally frustrated group had already presented their case to the government the previous spring. They were members of a recently inaugurated anti-prohibition organization calling itself People's Moderation Party (PMP). The party's choice of name was a clever one because it immediately cast its opponents—prohibitionists—as radicals.

The term "un-British," which Farris used to describe the PPA's proposal, was exactly how moderationists perceived prohibition itself. It was not a new argument. Leading up to the 1916 prohibition referendum, in public-relations campaigns waged between Vancouver's anti-prohibition

Merchant's Protective Association (MPA) and the PPA, an MPA newspaper advertisement had asked rhetorically, "Is it [potential prohibition] British? Is it consistent with the British principles of fair play?" Asked four years later, those same questions seemed more relevant than ever.

Since the turn of the century, BC had welcomed more British immigrants than any other province. By war's end, over 75 percent of the province's population was British. The proportion was even higher in Vancouver (over 85 percent) and likely a similar percentage in Victoria. Together, these two cities represented roughly half of the province's entire population. The moderationists' accusation of "un-British" resonated strongly, despite the fact that many of British background had democratically voted for prohibition in a very British manner. Most of those sharing British heritage also shared something else that distinguished them from the majority of prohibitionists: their religious affiliation.

In the US, the fast-growing moral reform movement was spearheaded by Methodists and Baptists, two of Protestantism's more fundamentalist denominations. Members of these and other evangelical churches had been passionate advocates for social change. This so-called social gospel advocated, among other causes, women's suffrage, the abolition of child labour and liquor prohibition. Sometimes-fiery sermonizing from the pulpits spilled outside churches and into meeting halls and auditoriums and, by the late 1800s, into the streets.

Before the Second World War, religion was the bedrock of society. Churches had enormous influence. A century ago, it wasn't government funding that built hospitals, schools and recreation centres, it was fundraising religious groups. In the late 1890s, the New Westminster local of the Women's Christian Temperance Union, a US-based reform group, financed the Woman's Hospital on Third Avenue, which admitted mothers and children. Churches—and in New Westminster's case, church-supported reformers—sometimes supervised or actively built the facilities they funded.

Many British Columbians had very little historical or religious connection with American Protestants and none at all with Methodists and Baptists. By 1921, 31 percent of BC residents considered themselves members of the Church of England in Canada, later called the Anglican Church. Anglicans and Roman Catholics eschewed fire-and-brimstone sermons for a predictable, contemplative church liturgy. On cue, members of the Anglican congregation knelt, rose or stood motionless, contained and restrained. Led by an unseen organist, they politely sang poetic hymns. There were none of the spontaneous hollers of joy heard in Baptist churches, no pounded pianos or jangled tambourines, none of the call-and-response inspired by a swaying, hand-clapping choir belting out fervent up-tempo gospel songs.

Outside their granite cathedrals, Anglicans and Roman Catholics avoided the public displays of emotionalism associated with prohibitionists. The Anglican Church had distrusted the concept of prohibition from the outset. In 1902, the prescient Anglican Synod had determined that "in remedying those [social] evils in one direction, we must be careful least we create others probably as great in another." Growing dissatisfaction with prohibition emphasized the gulf between BC's Anglican majority and the province's Methodist minority (merely 12 percent of residents) and the even smaller number of Baptists, who had trumpeted wartime prohibition in the first place. However, that war was over. Now, another war was about to begin, waged between peacetime prohibitionists and almost everyone else.

No moderationist personified "British" more than one of the PMP's staunchest supporters, Scottish-born Henry Bell-Irving. The pioneer industrialist had consolidated nine independent West Coast canneries into the mighty Anglo-British Columbia Packing Company, "the world's No. 1 producer of sockeye salmon." Bell-Irving's cannery empire gave him the kind of boardroom (and restaurant) table suasion needed to strengthen the PMP's position. He was the perfect choice to become party chairman.

Another PMP supporter was a former politician who brought invaluable insight to the organization. Thomas Walter Scott had served as the first premier of Saskatchewan. When he wasn't travelling, the retired Scott was living a life of ease in Victoria. Like former BC premier Richard McBride, Scott had been bedeviled by prohibitionists. However, the liquor strategies of Scott's Liberals were stunningly different than those of McBride's Conservatives. In March 1915, Saskatchewan residents went into shock when Scott personally announced that on July 1, the government would close every saloon in the province. But that was only the first step. It was Scott's second step that interested moderationists the most.

The Saskatchewan government hastily organized a network of government-controlled liquor "dispensaries," but no one needed a prescription to buy. In a single stroke, the Scott Liberals had changed everything. Drinking wouldn't be done in public saloons anymore; it would be done in private homes. Government outlets weren't located on every downtown street corner, either, as saloons had been. Only one had been planned for the city of Saskatoon. There were limits on how much a customer could buy and take home. Thus, the government controlled consumption. Through liquor testing, the government would also control quality. If prices for quality-assured liquor were reasonable, the government could limit the appeal of backwoods-still rotgut and perhaps control bootlegging and keep it from growing, which it would surely do under prohibition. As a third step, Scott agreed to hold a general plebiscite on liquor sometime in the future.

Saskatchewan "ban the bar" prohibitionists had applauded step one but decried step two. Local options allowed prohibitionists to vent their feelings. Seven districts opted to go to the ballot box, and by large majorities, residents in each of these districts voted the government dispensaries out. When prohibitionists forced the government to make good on its plebiscite pledge, Saskatchewan wets were doomed. Reform zeal—exemplified by prohibition and, presumably, the welfare of sons and fathers fighting in Flanders—would not be denied. Seventeen months of a severely restricted number of liquor outlets wasn't enough, and neither was province-wide quality control. Liquor was thrown onto wartime's sacrificial altar. On May 1, 1917, Saskatchewan went dry.

How terrible Scott's timing had been! Now the fervour of war—and the fear of food shortages—was over. Moreover, thousands of frustrated war veterans wanted whisky, rum and full-strength beer to flow legally again. In April 1920, a delegation boasting it represented 33,000 BC vets pleaded with Premier Oliver to end prohibition. The general public was disgusted, not so much by bootlegging as by prohibitionists' abuses and the government's inability to enforce its own law. With his own caucus wrangling over the issue, the premier—who had supported prohibition—was moved to comment, "I have lived long enough to know that prohibition cannot be enforced in British Columbia in the present state of public feeling."

Oliver's government saw a way out through the PMP. The party proposed, in essence, what Scott had undertaken in Saskatchewan: government control of liquor distribution and sales. The key was control, not prohibition. The moderationists also went further than Scott had done, proposing government-controlled public drinking, allowing at least a glass of wine or a beer with a restaurant meal.

That was the public profile of the moderationist philosophy. However, another philosophy was at work as well. At its heart was the desire to increase government revenues. If, even in prohibition, liquor revenues had provided over a half-million dollars of net profit to government coffers the year before, what might revenues be with legalized across-the-board liquor sales?

In early September, the government announced its solution. It wasn't, as the PPA proposed, turning government liquor enforcement over to the people; instead, a prohibition referendum would be held on October 1. People would be asked if they wanted prohibition to continue or if they supported a government-controlled alternative. Asking voters about public drinking was too big a leap for the government and, likely, for a public still wary of the long, dark shadow cast by saloons of the recent past. The PPA and PMP prepared for battle.

The PPA entered the fray beset by financial concerns. Their revenues for 1918 totalled a paltry $2,500 and made a mockery of the association's $10,000 budget. In another limit to beneficence, Jonathan Rogers was now charging rent for office space. To help install prohibition, leading businessmen, such as food manufacturer W.H. Malkin and retailer David Spencer, had made contributions and urged their customers to do the same. Now, W.G. Fortune admitted to Vancouver's innovative department-store magnate Charles Woodward, it was "more difficult to raise funds . . . than ever in the past. So many seemed carried away by the thought of government control."

What was carrying most people away, moderationists knew, was simply the thought of having a legal, high-quality drink or two at home before dinner. The PMP ran a consistent but low-key ad and door-to-door canvassing campaign stressing that prohibition was unenforceable and should be ended. Unlike the PPA, it organized no large rallies but held dozens of small meetings in halls and schools instead. At one school meeting, Captain Ian Mackenzie, MLA and president of the Vancouver branch of the Great War Veterans Association, said that 80 percent of returned soldiers would vote for repeal; they had fought tyranny on the Western Front and would fight it again in BC. As for women supporting prohibition, that was a myth, suggested a Victoria lady, referring to a repeal petition bearing the signatures of 8,000 women.

The PPA distributed tens of thousands of pamphlets and ran newspaper ads. "A Deluge of Booze!" warned one. But social perceptions had shifted. Was booze the cause of deep social problems—poverty, crime, prostitution, venereal disease—or was it merely a symptom of them? Like the PMP, the PPA reached out into the Okanagan, the Kootenays and the Cariboo, spreading its 20th-century version of the social gospel. Prairie firebrand Nellie McClung spoke at the Orpheum Theatre, insisting that "government control would be practically as bad as the days of the open bar."

In 1916, prohibitionists' margin of victory had been slim enough to suggest voter apathy played a role in defeating wets. Wets took no chances. "Apathy," a PMP *Vancouver Sun* ad announced, was "The Greatest Enemy of Freedom." This time around, the stakes were much higher than just legalizing liquor. What was at stake was the principal of democracy itself. The PMP urged citizens—wet or dry—to simply get out and vote. And they did.

Referendum results stunned the PPA. Prohibition had been overwhelmingly defeated by a majority of 35,437 votes. Only Chilliwack and Richmond voted dry. Even in Victoria, headquarters of the Women's Christian Temperance Union and where over 75 percent of eligible voters turned out, government control won by a two-to-one margin. On June 15, 1921, opening day for the first liquor stores, the *Vancouver Sun* reported, "At 11 a.m. today, the province of British Columbia enters the liquor business." The last province in the country to go dry was now the first English-speaking province to go wet again. Others would follow.

On the other side of the border that summer, attitudes were very different. It hadn't always been that way. Upon its eventual entry into the First World War, Americans, like Canadians, had understood the need to conserve foodstuffs at the expense of liquor. But instead of rationing restaurant meats, as Ottawa did, Washington, DC, closed distilleries. A Wartime Prohibition Act then outlawed winemaking and beer brewing, a bitter blow to the already-beleaguered brewing fraternity. Some big names—Anheuser-Busch, Blatz, F. & M. Schaefer, Schlitz and Pabst—and many smaller ones reflected their owners' German heritage. Capitalizing on centuries of Bavarian brewing tradition, beer barons had made family names the centerpiece of promotion and advertising. However, once US troops sailed off to fight "the Hun," anyone with a German name risked being the target of hate. Even when their social status shielded them from the more rabid demonstrators, many chose to disguise their origins. After moving from dry Seattle to wet San Francisco to brew Old German Lager, the Old German Lager Brewing Company decided to change both its corporate and brand names. New signage and letterhead announced Old Lager Brewing Company was now the home of Old Original Lager.

With peace declared, Washington, DC, abandoned "war emergency" prohibition, but 33 dry states did not. Using its growing influence, the mighty Anti-Saloon League (ASL) of America intimidated state politicians readying themselves for re-election. The ASL was too big for politicians to oppose, while on the other hand, espousing its dry cause improved the odds of an incumbent's election victory.

Americans had the opportunity to make national prohibition a success—or avoid it altogether. The object lessons were in the years of social, legal and law-enforcement upheaval in Washington and Oregon and other dry states, and in prohibition's obvious political and legal shortcomings north of the border. Yet, by 1919, there was no stopping the American prohibition juggernaut. Congress voted in the Constitution's 18th Amendment, making possible what Republican presidential candidate Herbert Hoover would later call "a great social and economic experiment, noble in motive, far-reaching in purpose."

"The reign of tears is over," Billy Sunday exulted. "The slums will soon only be a memory. We will turn our prisons into factories and our jails into storehouses and corncribs," he promised an audience of 10,000. "Men will walk upright now, women will smile and the children will laugh. Hell will be forever for rent."

When BC voted to repeal prohibition in October 1920, the disbelieving *Seattle Times* somehow concluded the province was simply "experimenting . . . in its progress toward bone-dry Prohibition." When they read the *New York Times'* front-page repeal story, east-coast residents likely wondered why Canada's west-coast province had abandoned the noble, far-reaching experiment. Of course, by then it was too late to do anything about it. In the face of a storm of social and political agitation to outlaw the sale of alcohol, the entire US had voted dry 10 months before.

7

Johnny and the Rum-Runners

AFTER HIS FIRST WHISKY RUN across the border in early November 1921, it's a wonder Victoria's Johnny Schnarr didn't give up on the whole business forever. A few days before, he'd been standing on an Inner Harbour wharf, staring at the 28-footer that liquor-man Harry was sure would make them rich. At that moment, Johnny worried the boat wasn't big enough to make the voyage down to San Francisco, but he would discover *Rose Marie* was more sea-worthy than Harry, despite the boasts of his would-be first mate. But the $500 captain's pay in his pocket helped him to overlook any potential risks. Just hours out of Victoria, while Johnny took a nap, helmsman Harry managed to steer *Rose Marie* in a circle, from Sooke harbour right back to the lights of Victoria. At this rate, Johnny figured, it might be a long voyage. He had no idea just how long.

When the engine quit, Johnny fixed it. When a storm hit, Johnny manoeuvred them into the protective (and dry-as-dust) Astoria. Why not just sell the booze here? Johnny asked. Harry was adamant that they continue on to San Francisco. After five days without sleep, Johnny finally turned the wheel and compass over to Harry to get some shut-eye. What could go wrong? Plenty, as it turned out. Offshore swells swamped the craft. Schnarr managed to run the sinking booze boat up on a deserted Oregon beach, where he and Harry stood watching the surf pound it to bits. If they worked quickly, Johnny figured, they might salvage the cargo.

"It was not a pleasant task, but it gave us something to do," Schnarr recalled in typical understated fashion, decades later. "We would climb on board between waves, let a breaker roll over us, then grab a sack of liquor each [bottles were transported in burlap sacks] and try to get ashore before the next wave hit." The exhausted pair managed to retrieve enough bottles to fill 70 cases out of the original 110 and, by 4 AM, had managed to hide them from scavenging beach-combers. However, the *Rose Marie* misadventure had only just begun.

Johnny told four farmers about their hidden cache. The farmers agreed to haul the liquor away and sell it, but they hijacked it instead. Johnny and Harry were then apprehended by Prohibition agents and spent the night in jail. In a moment of classic irony, a local sheriff actually offered Johnny $250 to help him catch the pirates who had stolen the liquor. Pirates were dangerous, so as broke as he was, Johnny declined the offer. The two penniless Canadians finally had some money wired down to Oregon, then boarded a bus and headed north, with Johnny figuring he was lucky "to have got out of the whole mess with my skin."

While Harry rolled on back to BC, Schnarr stopped at Chehalis, Washington, and picked up where he had left off as a logging-camp faller. Then, he received a letter from Fred Kohse, the Victoria friend who had urged him to embark on his initial rum-running misadventure. "This time he wanted me to operate a boat for him running loads of liquor across the Strait of Juan de Fuca," Johnny recalled, landing it on deserted beaches near Anacortes, Washington, for pickup. This sounded sensible, and Johnny quit the logging camp. This time he would do it right, and he would do it over and over again, for more than 400 runs during 12 years of US Prohibition.

By the spring of 1921, German-born Kohse and US-born Schnarr had known each other almost 10 years. They weren't exactly two peas in a pod, but they were off the same vine, both multi-talented and adventurous. The two had met before the First World War in the coastal BC wilderness. Logging all summer and trapping all winter near Bute Inlet with his two brothers, Johnny knew how to rough it. He also knew boating. "We didn't think anything of rowing twenty or thirty miles in a day," Johnny remembered. Those youthful experiences taught Johnny how to be resourceful, especially at repairing motors. As he and his brothers also discovered, Johnny had a knack for building canoes. "I seemed to have the best eye for the lines the boat should have," he recalled.

Johnny's hunting and trapping years also made him a keen marksman, bagging "at least thirty cougar" with his brother for the bounty. Johnny later ranked ninth in shooting in America's overseas army of 2 million men.

Some men get into a comfortable rut, but not Fred Kohse. When he met Johnny, the former Empress Hotel head waiter was travelling the coastal inlets with his wife, anxious to stake timber claims. He was also the operator of a boathouse, maintaining clients' boats and running tours up Victoria's Gorge waterway in the summer. Fred convinced Johnny to take over the boathouse, and before Johnny left BC for basic military training at Fort Lewis, he had learned how to take an inoperative boat engine apart, fix it and put it back together, and how to operate a powerboat on the open ocean.

In 1921, Fred made a couple of liquor runs across the Strait of Juan de Fuca himself, but he realized his first love was still shore-based, maintaining boats and making deals. Johnny would make the runs with Fred's brother-in-law, Billy Garrard, who would help load and unload. Things had changed in a big way since the *Rose Marie* trip five months before. Johnny Schnarr had joined an elite fraternity of mostly young men who split profits with boat-owning deal makers. Johnny's share was two-thirds, which he then split with Billy. They made their runs either hugging the outer shoreline or speeding down Puget Sound to points just north of the Seattle–Tacoma area.

This particular fleet had no single commander; there were dozens of individual "admirals." No overall battle plan existed in this theatre of the whisky war. Skippers of single boats acted completely independently from their colleagues. Sometimes—like Schnarr—the skipper was the boat's owner. Most often, the boats had been purchased or built by individuals known collectively under such corporate names as General Navigation Company of Canada, Pacific and Foreign Navigation Company and Arctic Traders. Triangle Freighters, in liquor-trade irony, rented its office space in the stately downtown Vancouver building owned by the very personification of BC's struggle for prohibition, Jonathan Rogers. It's doubtful that the former PPA president realized a tenant in the Rogers Building represented the kind of men who had destroyed prohibition, his heartfelt cause.

Most rum-trade skippers were not colleagues in the usual sense of the word, and there was little fraternizing while ashore. Trust was rare; suspicion ruled. This tight-lipped attitude is one reason why so little verifiable information on the trade is available today. At a farewell party of the "Brethren of the [Rum] Row" held in the fo'c's'le galley of the fish-packer *Shuchona*, Jack Harwood, captain of the rum-running fishboat *Ruth B*, proposed a toast: "We must never forget the brethren's motto, 'Don't never tell nothin' to nobody, nohow.'"

On his first trip, Johnny was instructed to run *Rose Marie* south of Victoria and make a starboard turn into isolated little Pedder Bay to load liquor. For the next few trips, Johnny and Billy simply transferred 75 cases of liquor stacked up on the dock below Victoria's Wharf Street into Kohse's little boats. There was no secrecy; the heavy wooden cases were just rolled out from Consolidated Exporters, on the corner of Wharf and Fort Streets. Loading wasn't a silent, stealthy operation made in the dead of night, either; it was done in broad daylight on the bustling waterfronts of Victoria and Vancouver. Prohibition repeal had made what these rum-runners were doing perfectly legal—on the Canadian side of the border. In fact, the 19-dollar export duty on each case transported south of the line—a duty that would increase as time went by—had Canadian customs officials and Ottawa politicians smiling all the while. Very soon, Johnny was smiling, too.

After one month, Johnny Schnarr was in the money. Six trips made him $1,000, seven times what a typical office wage slave took home every month. It was nice to buy a bottle of whisky or rum legally again, but the real impact of prohibition's repeal was the money generated in the fast-growing rum-running sector. The trickle-down effect extended to hundreds of Vancouver and Victoria men who never sniffed salt water: warehouse workers, truckers, boat-builders, machine-shop metal benders, equipment dealers, mechanics, electricians—and real-estate representatives, too.

Property-purchasing "exporters" helped keep recession-strapped Victoria's new Uplands development afloat. In 1931, near the city's Telegraph Bay, one particularly spacious two-storey home was built with rum-running profits. Owner Johnny Schnarr loved the secluded oceanfront location. He could moor his newest shoreboat, *Kitnayakwa*, just 500 feet from his newly constructed house. A few months later, in Vancouver, liquor mogul George Reifel used rum-running proceeds to help complete a 21,000-square-foot Spanish colonial revival–style mansion on southwest Marine Drive. Casa Mia featured a billiard room, lounge and an art-deco ballroom complete with sprung dance floor and a stage where jazz greats Louis Armstrong, Duke Ellington and Count Basie later performed. Because they were denied rooms at high-end downtown hotels, the legendary bandleaders and their musicians slept upstairs in some of Casa Mia's eight bedrooms. Seventy-five years after the Reifels moved in, the asking price for the home was $12 million.

By the end of US Prohibition, the trade had involved around 100 boats. Some, such as the former lighthouse tender *Quadra*, were full-sized ships. The 175-foot, 683-ton steel-hulled steamer chugged sedately down the outer coast as far as California. On her last voyage, *Quadra* reportedly carried a cargo worth a half-million dollars, cases of high-quality liquor below and dozens of barrels of whisky on deck. The small, slow boats Johnny Schnarr initially piloted for Fred Kohse had limited carrying capacity. Schnarr and other skippers worried that the US Coast Guard would soon increase its vigilance, perhaps with newer, faster, better-armed vessels. Cargo size was irrelevant if the rum-runner was apprehended. Speed, not capacity, became the priority.

Johnny called her *Moonbeam*. She began as a three-foot wooden model with a high-speed hull, which Johnny carved himself. He showed the model to the Yonedas, a Japanese father-son shipwright team in Victoria. Although Scharr hadn't planned it, *Moonbeam* would be a prototype of the "shore boat" or "fireboat" (short for "firewater boat"), the sleek, low-profiled, high-powered kind of motorboat that would dominate 1920s coastal rum-running. *Moonbeam*'s construction was timely; the new boat was half-finished when Kohse decided he wanted a bigger cut, leaving Johnny and Billy with less. Both quit. Then, two Seattle bootleggers, Carl Melby and Pete Peterson, who had waited for Johnny on some of those deserted Puget Sound beaches, paid the rum-runner a visit. The liquor-traffic grapevine had tipped them that Johnny was building a boat. When it's ready, let us know, they told him. Soon, Johnny Schnarr was at the throttles again, this time in business for himself as Fred Kohse's newest competitor.

To save money, Johnny installed a Marmon automobile engine he had chosen himself. Johnny's clever engine choice enabled *Moonbeam* to move at up to 18 knots, enough to leave a 12-knot Coast Guard cutter behind. The new boat's maximum loads—purchased by Melby and Peterson from Consolidated Exporters—were just 75 cases, small enough to load into the bootleggers' two cars, a slightly modified Cadillac and Studebaker. *Moonbeam* would be the first vessel of a small fleet Johnny Schnarr designed and had built. Each boat needed to be faster than the previous one to keep a step ahead of larger and faster US Coast Guard vessels.

By 1924, Seattle's Lake Union dry dock had won the tender to construct 15 new 75-foot Coast Guard "rum-chasers." America's "dry navy" continued to expand. Sliding down the shipyard ways after the 75-foot "six-bitter" cutters were 100-foot "dollar" boats and 125-foot, heavily armed "dollar-and-a-quarter" vessels.

The boating magazines Johnny Schnarr was reading featured ads for 300-horsepower Fiat aircraft engines. Johnny bought one, and when he finished installing it, *Moonbeam* became, in his own words, "the fastest boat around at the time." *Moonbeam* was fast enough that Johnny managed to evade the Coast Guard cutter *Arcata*, which fired at the fast-moving shoreboat several times as Johnny sped away. But as good as *Moonbeam* was, Johnny Schnarr decided he needed something bigger.

The bigger boat the Yonedas built for Johnny was *Miss Victoria*, a 48-footer with a 9-foot beam. Again, the timing was good. While Johnny was in Seattle on a short holiday (and attending a big party hosted by Pete Peterson), Billy Garrard and a deckhand made a run down Puget Sound in *Moonbeam*. A Coast Guard cutter loomed out of nowhere. The boys made a run for it. Warning shots became deadly shots aimed right at the boat. Bullets struck the engine, and *Moonbeam*'s speed dropped. The two rum-runners managed to beach the craft. Screaming and cursing, "We've got you now, you sons of bitches!" the cutter's crew opened up with automatic rifle fire, riddling *Moonbeam*. They failed to notice the two Canadians dashing for the trees. A bus and CPR boat ride later, they were back in Victoria giving Johnny the bad news: *Moonbeam* was history.

The financial backing for Johnny's new boats illustrated just how much of a big-money business rum-running had become. When *Miss Victoria* hit the water, she was powered by two Fiat aircraft engines. As affluent as he was, Johnny didn't have enough money for two engines, but he knew he could get it from Pete Marinoff, an Olympia beer baron and bootlegger. Johnny told him he needed $3,000, and Marinoff "calmly peeled off thirty one-hundred dollar bills" and handed them to Johnny. "Pay me back when you can," Pete smiled, and then added, "I'll have some work for you when you get that new boat going." Marinoff needed Johnny. He had just lost two cargoes and a boat to the Coast Guard. Business was so good that Marinoff had his money back in six months.

Two other boats came and went, and then Johnny designed *Revuocnav* (Vancouver, spelled backwards), which was large enough to deliver merchandise for up to five customers at one time. Schnarr couldn't carry the cost alone. He put up $7,000 of his own money, and the "big boys" at Consolidated Exporters, who had urged him to build the boat, loaned him $15,000 for two 860-horsepower Packard engines. Consolidated received 40 percent of the fee for every delivery until the loan was repaid. In less than a year, Johnny was debt free, piloting a sleek, hydroplane-hulled craft he described as "all I dreamed a boat should be."

During 12 years of rum-running, Johnny Schnarr survived enough escapades to fill a book, which he eventually dictated to his niece, Marion Parker, 50 years later. "I'm always amazed that more people weren't killed," he told Marion. Schnarr came close to meeting his maker more than once. While carrying for Peterson and Melby one night in 1923, the rum-runner didn't realize how narrowly he had escaped being cut down until days later. At Anacortes, where Washington State ferries would dock in the future, Billy Garrard rowed cases to and from the lonely beach in the shoreboat's skiff and helped bootleggers load their cars. Suddenly, lights lit up the cove. Johnny saw everything from *Moonbeam's* deck. "Melby and Billy ran one way with two of the policemen in hot pursuit, while Pete Peterson ran the other ... cops firing at them with handguns."

Johnny then realized one of the dry agents standing on the gravel was shooting at *Moonbeam* repeatedly with a rifle and—it seemed—missing. "I had to believe that he really didn't want to hit her," Johnny figured. Then, the rifleman dashed into the trees after Billy and the bootleggers. Johnny waited a few minutes and then headed back to Victoria with what was left of the load. A few days later, he heard the rest of the story. Melby had taken a bullet in the sole of his left foot. When police gave up the chase, breathless Billy Garrard had pried the protruding slug out of the bootlegger's foot with his pocket knife. The two men had met Pete Peterson and his Cadillac at a prearranged spot and drove off. Later, Melby told police his Studebaker had been stolen, and he simply visited the police station to pick it up. Cars were intact, nobody had been killed or even seriously hurt, and all Consolidated Exporters had lost was 30 cases of booze. All Johnny lost was an easily replaced skiff.

A few months later, on the west side of Whidbey Island, Seattle agents were waiting once again (likely tipped off by Peterson and Melby's competitors), and "bullets were flying left, right and centre." Billy simply cut the anchor line and the rum-runners sped away into the darkness. The next morning, friendly George Norris, the chief customs inspector, walked down the wharf at Victoria's Inner Harbour and took a very close look at *Moonbeam*. He had received a call from the Seattle feds. Johnny had examined the boat over on Discovery Island, where he and Billy had spent the night and had found nothing. Now, in stunned silence, he watched Norris dig a slug out of *Moonbeam*'s stern. Customs impounded the boat.

Johnny and the Rum-Runners

While rum-runners faced the very real risks of sudden storms, unpredictable swells, hull-destroying deadheads, vicious hijackers and potentially lethal gunfire from shore and Coast Guard patrols, the very least of rum-runners' worries was US or Canadian law. A potential criminal charge meant next to nothing; Johnny figured he could beat this conviction since it was based on such flimsy evidence. Yet he also realized "it could have kept the boat tied up for several months at least." So, two weeks later, when orders started to come in, Johnny decided "it was simpler just to pay the 500-dollar fine and go back to work."

Johnny Schnarr's biggest, fastest boat, *Kitnayakwa*, took bullets, too, on a night when Johnny came perilously close to stopping some himself. The night was so dark, only a bow swell's phosphorescence warned Johnny a Coast Guard cutter had closed in about 100 feet astern. Orange-red tracer bullets from the cutter's machine guns began to speed through the darkness, one flashing between Johnny and his open-mouthed assistant standing just two feet away. Johnny hit the throttles. *Kitnayakwa*'s two Liberty aircraft engines allowed the rum-runners to evade another five cutters that fateful night. Eighteen bullet holes had been punched into the hull and cabin housing. To avoid another Canadian Customs seizure, Johnny and others worked for hours to fill in and disguise every bullet hole.

8

The Men of Rum Row

SOME 12 MILES EAST FROM Johnny Schnarr and his fellow shoreboat skippers, the heavily laden ships of the Pacific's Rum Row rolled placidly at anchor in international waters off northern California and Mexico, waiting for the customers to venture out to them. Washington, Oregon and California bootleggers—and, occasionally, members of the shore-hugging fireboat fleet—arrived to load up their contraband cargo from a motley armada of engine-augmented two- or three-masted schooners, steam freighters, former ore carriers, yachts, fish packers and First World War sub-chasers. The stationary fleet grew quickly, from just 4 ships in 1922 to 25 vessels at the height of activity a decade later. Rum Row represented the smaller of the two fleets, but in terms of income, it vastly outweighed its shoreboat counterpart. Rum Row meant huge profits for men who seldom—if ever— ventured out beyond the swimming beaches of Vancouver's English Bay and Oak Bay's Willows Beach.

The cargo capacity of the vessels varied. Fully loaded, the low-slung, 94-foot sub-chaser *Ragna* shipped 1,800 cases of liquor; by contrast, the enormous five-masted schooner *Malahat* had room in her holds for over 80,000 cases. Exporters often had more cases stacked up topside, until the decks barely cleared the waterline. There were thirsty people in Alaska, too, so *Malahat* sometimes dropped anchor off northern Cape Flattery, allowing the fish-packer *Kiltuish* to load 10,000 cases. Then *Malahat* sailed south. Even her mammoth holds soon emptied out. Smaller boats puttered up to resupply the huge schooner and other ships. One was a Prince Rupert halibut schooner, *Chief Skugaid*. Thanks to US Prohibition, her deckhands were making the richest "catches" of their lives—and no more tossing about in a dory in a heavy chop.

Once a mother ship got into position, the crew simply waited for customers. Yet the larger operation was far from simple. It required dealing with hard-bargaining US customers and bloody-minded skippers, taking delivery of merchandise, loading ships, arranging customs clearances and then getting vessels to designated positions and back again safely. The row itself was just one component of a well-oiled machine fuelled by big money and operated, in the main, by a handful of seasoned liquor men and mariners. Through their distribution companies, agents sought out buyers (bootleggers) and made cash transactions, often arriving back in BC carrying hundreds of thousands of dollars in cash, small fortunes in the Roaring Twenties.

The Victoria facility supplying Johnny Schnarr was actually a branch operation. Headquartered in Vancouver at a Hamilton Street warehouse that held thousands of cases of liquor, Consolidated Exporters was created by a group of Canadian brewers and hotelmen determined to cash in on US Prohibition. It wasn't hard to source the best product; by US Prohibition's start, Ottawa had rescinded the wartime ban on liquor transportation. Boxcars full of Corby's and Wiser's were continually rolling west from Ontario. While other Wharf Street operations such as Rithet Consolidated (exporting King George IV Scotch whisky) and Pither and Leiser (warehousing Teacher's Scotch whisky in what is now the Dogwood Building) joined Consolidated in quenching American thirsts, another group was building a three-storey distillery on Texada Island's Pocahontas Bay.

By the onset of US Prohibition, the name Henry Reifel was a familiar one. The American immigrant and his brother had established a Vancouver brewery almost 40 years before. By the First World War, Reifel was operating three breweries. Back in BC after a successful prohibition-era period brewing rice beer in Japan, neither Henry nor his son George could ignore a nationwide prohibition opportunity. The family

A former US Navy First World War sub-chaser, *Hickey* became a rum-runner in the coastal whisky wars. Like other "shoreboats," *Hickey* had enough engine power to outrun Coast Guard cutters.
VANCOUVER MARITIME MUSEUM

family purchased BC Distillery in New Westminster, built another distillery in Ontario and established Pacific Forwarding as their Pacific-region distribution arm. The Reifel family did more than rely on rum-runners and the men on the row; it operated boats of its own, including Johnny Schnarr's former *Miss Victoria II.*

BC liquor exporters' most significant client wasn't an individual but the Seattle bootlegging ring Western Freighters, owners of a three-masted schooner, *Pescawha,* a sleek, modern freighter, *Prince Albert,* and at least two fireboats that raced cargo from its bigger vessels down Puget Sound. Western Freighters was operated by former

Seattle police lieutenant Roy Olmstead, who had been thrown off the force in 1920 after being identified unloading liquor from a tugboat. His dismissal merely allowed Olmstead to devote his full attention to liquor interests, and he quickly took the bootlegging crown that Jack Marquett and the Billingsley brothers had once fought for. Occasionally, Olmstead combined business with pleasure, cruising over the border in his speedboat, *Zambesie*, to pick up 100 cases of liquor on picturesque D'Arcy Island.

By 1922, the business had become so big that bootleggers staged their own well-publicized Seattle convention, where they fixed the per-case retail price and even established a contingency fund to offset arrest and prosecution expenses. In order to ensure the best wholesale prices, the "bottle men" decided to play off dozens of Canadian exporters against each other by buying more booze originating from Victoria.

More and more often, US Coast Guard cutters hovered near the mother ships, making it impossible for *Malahat* and others to off-load liquor to frustrated customers. However, that was a mere nuisance compared to the fates of two Canadian ships. In late 1924, the Coast Guard cutter *Shawnee* made a big catch. Accounts differed: Had *Quadra* strayed into US waters? Had she just collided with *Malahat* off California while loading liquor from that floating warehouse? Was *Quadra* taking on water when *Shawnee* fired a round across her bow? What mattered more than the details was that *Shawnee*'s captain, Charles F. Howell, had his prize

The ill-fated *Quadra* may have been seized in international waters. Just a few months before she left Vancouver under a Union Jack, Britain and the US signed a new treaty. The US Coast Guard could board, search and seize a liquor vessel anywhere, and "His Britannic Majesty agrees he will raise no objection." VANCOUVER MARITIME MUSEUM

towed into San Francisco, where what was left of *Quadra*'s cargo was seized along with her sales proceeds.

The early 1925 attack on the mother ship *Coal Harbour* was similar to the one launched against *Quadra*. *Coal Harbour*'s skipper had once faced more deadly attacks. A decorated First World War hero, Charles Hudson served aboard the famed British Q-boats, the discreetly but heavily armed merchant ships that lured German submarines into ill-fated surface combat. According to Hudson, *Coal Harbour* was clearly outside US territorial limits, so when an officer of the Coast Guard's *Cahokia* bawled "Heave to for boarding!" Hudson replied "No dice!" and manoeuvred *Coal Harbour* away. This clumsy game of catch me if you can continued until, as Hudson told it, "They first got two men aboard us, then seven and finally a dozen, who took the tow line and started us into San Francisco." In Hudson's view, his ship had been taken illegally in international waters. The Americans' view was that 7,000 bottles of liquor inside *Coal Harbour*'s hold was reason enough to take her in.

After at least one night in jail, Hudson left his confiscated ship behind to rust at the jetty. Back in Vancouver, he resumed his more important vocation—"marine superintendent" of General Navigation Company of Canada and Rithet Consolidated in Victoria. Hudson ran Rum Row from Hamilton Street and from home, where a radio set linked him with the mother ships through men wearing earphones who were nicknamed—inevitably—Sparks or Sparky.

A similar fate befell Western Freighters' *Pescawha*, set to off-load liquor at the mouth of the Columbia. This time the circumstances were ironic and the finale tragic. Through his binoculars, *Pescawha* skipper Robert Pamphlett saw a derelict ship tossing close to the rocky shore and then spied a small, open boat. Fearful of hijackers, he ordered members of his crew to arm themselves. Lying on the deck, crewmen pointed rifles at what now appeared to be a lifeboat from the abandoned ship. *Pescawha* rescued its crew and captain, who commented that *Pescawha*'s men "treated us like kings. Everything on board was ours."

Then *Pescawha*'s good-luck rescue went bad. Pamphlett unwisely tarried just six and a half miles offshore for four hours. Spying the Coast Guard's *Algonquin*, he then tried to make for international waters. A shot across *Pescawha*'s bows brought her to a halt. When Pamphlett turned the rescued sailors over to *Algonquin* and wished them all a safe journey home, perhaps he expected *Algonquin*'s captain, in high-seas tradition, to salute the gallant rum-runner and continue on its way. Instead, *Algonquin* ignobly towed the US-owned *Pescawha* into Portland.

Pamphlett's fate wasn't so felicitous. While extradition was only a remote possibility, the captain did the honourable thing, returning to Portland to be tried and sentenced. That was Pamphlett's final, fatal mistake. Despite, as the *Vancouver Sun* put it, risking "his life and his freedom to rescue American sailors in peril" and the petitions mounted on his behalf by Americans (who awarded him a gold watch for his actions), and despite lobbying efforts by Attorney General Alexander Manson in Ottawa, Pamphlett spent a year in McNeil Island prison. The sentence cost him more than time; it cost him his health. Pamphlett contracted tuberculosis and died two years after his release, at age 58.

Shawnee's captain, Charles Howell, put on a fitting spit-and-polish courtroom show when he and members of his crew helped convict *Quadra*'s captain, George Ford, and members of his crew. Ford's sentence was two years behind bars and a $1,000 fine. In the prosecutor's words, Howell's "clean cut, fine appearance . . . reflected great credit on the coast guard and the government." Rascally Captain Ford and his crewmen soon jumped bail and slipped north across the border. Sometime later, BC's rum-runners, who were masterful at appearing innocent when encountering the Coast Guard ("Just doin' a bit of cruising, Lieutenant"), were probably not surprised to learn that Howell was back in court, on trial for perjury. One of Consolidated Exporters' competitors had paid Howell $20,000 to apprehend *Quadra* anywhere he could find her and an additional 20 grand to keep quiet about it. Howell's Coast Guard career was over.

When the Coast Guard appeared unable to stop the tide of liquor lapping onto US shores, America trained its big gun on Canadian rum-runners. The weapon wasn't the one-pounder mounted on a Coast Guard cutter's bow. It was high-powered political pressure from Washington, DC. By 1929, Ottawa had passed a new law. Early in US Prohibition, nobody inside the two-storey stone customs building on Wharf Street really cared where liquor cargo eventually ended up, as long as it went—officially—anywhere but the US. Now they cared. A liquor ship couldn't slip out of Vancouver, sit on Rum Row and come back to Vancouver empty anymore. Liquor ships headed for a formally designated foreign port actually had to discharge their cargoes at that port. To do otherwise was breaking a Canadian law.

Few rum-runners were loading up in broad daylight below Wharf Street now. Instead, Consolidated loaded slow-moving fishing boats that chugged their way to Saturna, D'Arcy or Discovery Island, the most southerly of BC's Gulf Islands. There, rum-runners would transfer loads to their small boats and speed down the coast. The ever-wary Johnny Schnarr had stopped loading up in Victoria's Inner Harbour years before. Discreet Discovery Island had long been his port of call for cargo.

Eventually the US west-coast market attracted Canada's most infamous liquor men, 2,000 miles away. Since dry US ports were out of bounds, and most Mexican fishing villages didn't have facilities, Vancouver moguls managing Rum Row decided to make Papeete, Tahiti, their official port of call. Setting up warehousing and merchandise control in the Polynesian paradise would take big money. Consolidated and Pacific Forwarding found it in Montreal, where the Bronfman brothers were counting their rum-running fortunes.

Rum Row was a familiar concept to the Bronfmans; they had been supplying the east-coast version of it for years. In 1922 alone, their warehouse inventory on the French-held island of St. Pierre was valued at more than $1 million. The Bronfmans had the bucks west-coasters needed. Once a sales agent was running things on Tahiti, ships were coming and going constantly. At one point, the inventory of Canadian and Scotch whiskies, gins, American bourbons, European champagnes and liqueurs warehoused beneath the palm trees was worth over $1.2 million wholesale.

CHAPTER

9

Pacific Coast Pirates

GROWING UP IN PUGET SOUND, the Eggers boys—Milo (Micky), Theodore (Ted) and Ariel (Happy)—had it good. Sons of a successful seafood wholesaler, they were probably used to getting what they wanted. As they matured, they wanted more, and they knew they weren't going to get it wearing a fishmonger's apron or even an owner's three-piece suit. Growing up during state prohibition, they had probably heard about the notorious Billingsley brothers. When the nation went dry, the Eggers boys began rum-running, retailing 20-dollar cases of whisky for over $200 each; however, Roy Olmstead's price-cutting crippled their business. Likely recalling rum-runner Jack Marquett, the Eggers brothers decided that the most effective way to undercut

Olmstead and other competitors was to mimic pirate Jack and avoid paying anything for their inventory.

When the Eggers boys' new motorboat *M-197* pulled up alongside *Pauline* in the spring of 1923, skipper Tom Avery was a happy man. Here was the shoreboat he was waiting for, moving up quickly to load his liquid merchandise. Except, as the *M-197* bumped alongside, Avery realized it wasn't the boat he had been expecting. Avery wasn't expecting guns pointed at his chest, either. Minutes later, the hijackers roared away with Avery's 128 cases of booze.

"Coffee's on. Come aboard," the smiling skipper of *Erskine* told the Eggers brothers, just a short time later. They slurped the captain's brew and then pulled their guns. The pirates commandeered *Erskine*, stashing half her load on Dungeness Island, and stacked the rest onto the *M-197* before vanishing over the horizon. Profits aside, what made the *Erskine* and *Pauline* heists so sweet was that the hijacked merchandise belonged to Roy Olmstead. The brothers' initial heists went smoothly, and they earned an overnight reputation as tough Pacific-coast pirates.

The brothers experienced the downside of their new-found notoriety when they manoeuvred close to the supply boat *Emma* and watched Captain Emery step on deck with an automatic pistol in each hand. The Eggers boys bluffed their way aboard, begging for the warmth of Emery's cabin and his coffee. They convinced Emery to let them stay overnight on his boat, hoping desperately he would nod off. He didn't. In the morning, they jumped into *M-197*, waved Emery goodbye and left empty-handed. The Eggers brothers soon received another very broad hint of what was to come.

After tying up near Discovery Island's lodge, two visitors started asking questions about liquor prices. One of the rum-runners they questioned got suspicious when the two "hawk-faced and raw-boned" characters didn't seem interested in buying any liquor. Their boat, *M-197*, also appeared faster than his employer's craft. After lunch, there was gunfire at the water's edge. The two newcomers and others were shooting at empty bottles bobbing in the shallows.

The suspicious rum-runner, Johnny Schnarr, decided to retrieve his handgun from Kohse's boat and join the fun. It'd been a long while since Johnny had actually shot anything, but he gamely aimed his German luger and let fly. *Bang, bang, bang!* The shards from three shattered bottles sank out of sight. "A bit lucky," he later admitted. Schnarr's luck held later that afternoon, when he and Billy Garrard spotted *M-197* following behind their heavily loaded boat. But *M-197* soon disappeared. "Perhaps they thought they might pick us off before going after the big haul [a bigger liquor shipment farther north] and then decided against it," Schnarr concluded. "I always liked to think that the little demonstration of my shooting skill probably helped them change their minds."

In the spring of 1924, a previous Eggers hijack victim, skipper Adolf Ongstad, lay just off North Pender Island in *Hadsel*, ready to transfer liquor to the American rum-runner *Kayak*. Ongstad and his crew relaxed when they spotted the familiar figure of Troy Martin on the deck of the approaching shoreboat. The boats were just 20 feet from each other when rifle fire sent Ongstad and his crew sprawling. One of Ongstad's crewmen cried out, clutching a bullet wound.

Four masked hijackers had earlier intercepted *Kayak* and forced one of its crewmen, Troy Martin, on deck to deceive Ongstad. By the end of the escapade, the crews of both boats stood helplessly aboard *Kayak* watching *Hadsel* and its 226 cases of liquor disappear south. Once again, the hijackers' unseen victim was Roy Olmstead. Olmstead wanted to know the identities of the thieves even more than the victimized rum-runners did. The Eggers brothers' reputation made them the number-one suspects. With things getting hot, they left Seattle for San Francisco. Other hijackers would soon take their place in the island-dotted waters.

Six months after the loss of *Kayak*'s load, bootlegger Pete Marinoff was nervously pacing a Puget Sound wharf, waiting for liquor off-loaded from *Beryl G*, a father-and-son-operated workboat. Marinoff was troubled because the Coast Guard had recently snared one of his newer boats. To add insult to injury, Assistant Prohibition Director William Whitney had commandeered the boat, and agents had used it to cruise the sound. Worse, Marinoff learned they also knew the craft was his. Quick payoffs had been arranged through a customs broker in Marinoff's pocket, and after payment of a light fine, the boat had been released. Marinoff's nervousness increased as he watched his shoreboat approach. She was riding too high in the water for a loaded boat. The reason was soon obvious: her holds were empty. The crew hadn't been able to locate *Beryl G*. The Canadian boat had vanished—and with it, 225 cases of valuable liquor.

Chris Waters, lighthouse keeper on tiny Stuart Island, one of the most northern of Washington State's San Juan Islands, knew exactly where *Beryl G* was. He was watching the deserted vessel rocking closer and closer to the rocks beneath his light. Here was a salvage opportunity. He hurried off to inform island postmaster Eric Erikson, whose boat could take *Beryl G* in tow. Within minutes of climbing aboard *Beryl G*, Waters and Erikson knew the vessel hadn't simply slipped its moorings. It wasn't the cabin's untidiness that captured their attention, it was the blood. It was smeared on a magazine, inside a mariner's cap, on the cabin floorboards, in the companionway, on the deck and on clothing found near the bow. *Beryl G* was a death ship. She made her last voyage at the end of a US Coast Guard cutter tow rope, destined for San Juan Island's Friday Harbor, where she awaited Canadian authorities.

The worried wife and daughter of *Beryl G* skipper William Gillis weren't much help to American authorities. Both were vague about the boat's cargo and destination— perhaps some nameless logging camp, they thought. Daughter

The rum-running death ship *Beryl G* tied up in Victoria's inner harbour during the investigation of its missing skipper, William Gillis, and his teenage son, Bill. VANCOUVER MARITIME MUSEUM

Beryl (after whom the boat was named) inadvertently told a *Bellingham Herald* reporter more when she visited to discuss the salvage claim by opportunists Waters and Erikson, who wanted one-third of the boat's value. Beryl said she feared her dad and 17-year-old brother Bill had been killed by "liquor pirates."

Roy Olmstead talked to newspaper reporters too: "We owe it not only to Captain Gillis but to the wife and family of every man in the trade to rid the seas of such ruthless pirates," he proclaimed, "and we will do it." While Olmstead's sympathies for the Gillis family may have been genuine, there was another motivation at work. Nobody needed to ask what "trade" Olmstead was referring to, nor who "we" meant. Olmstead needed the hijackers stopped. Ironically, the man who helped BC lawmen finally do it was one of Olmstead's competitors.

When BCPP inspector Forbes Cruickshank left his superintendent's office, he knew more about *Beryl G* than did the public, but not much. Cruickshank hadn't seen the boat, but a BCPP corporal had. The superintendent handed Cruickshank the report. The inspector likely wasn't thrilled to be burdened with this long-shot investigation so soon after his last one.

One of Vancouver's most notorious crime cases had gone badly before Cruickshank was involved and went worse afterward. There was a body (the nanny of an upper-class Shaughnessy Heights family), a weapon (a rusty revolver, lying conveniently beside the body) and the arrest of a suspect (a blood-smeared Chinese houseboy). Despite all this, the case had ended without a conviction. Was the nanny murdered? Did she commit suicide? The failure to answer that question and others—including accusations of police torture—prompted the grand jury to find "lack of evidence" and set the houseboy free. Cruickshank needed a break, but this case wasn't likely to provide it. He had even less evidence this time around.

Despite dragging the waters, no bodies had been found, nor a murder weapon—if, indeed, murders had been committed. What the inspector did have were bullet holes in the hull and the cabin door, rifle cartridges, shotgun shells and a missing anchor. Lawmen had produced a photo from a loaded camera discovered on *Beryl G.* It showed a boat's stern with the registration number *M-493*. Cruickshank started there.

The first break came inside the Lake Union lock keeper's office. A quick look through the files confirmed that *M-493* had passed through the locks between the lake and Puget Sound. The lock keeper also confirmed the boat belonged to somebody named Pete Marinoff. When Cruickshank showed Marinoff the photo, the bootlegger was initially defensive, asking what the photo proved. Very little, Cruickshank agreed. But Marinoff realized that, quite by accident, he had been given an opportunity to strike back at hijackers.

With the promise of immunity, Marinoff provided a carefully edited version of reality that didn't confirm much but gave Cruickshank a solid connection between rum-running and hijackers. It appeared that Gillis's daughter had been correct in her assumption. Marinoff tipped Cruickshank to Seattle garage operator Al Clausen. Cruickshank told Clausen he didn't care about rum-running or bootleggers, but this was murder. Murder was Canada's business, and it was a hanging business. The nervous Clausen began to talk.

Yes, Clausen had piloted his boat for some men a couple of times, picking up island-stashed liquor, liquor sometimes rebagged by a Pender Island farmer into sacks bearing green-painted Cs. The inspector demanded names and got them: Harry Sowash, Owen "Cannonball" Baker and Charlie Morris. Clausen blurted out something else, too. Baker had told Clausen that 50 sacks of booze picked up from a cache at a cove near Anacortes had come from "the old man and the boy."

Cruickshank prodded. Who did Clausen think Baker was talking about?

"I thought it was Captain Gillis and son off the *Beryl G*," Clausen told him.

Cruickshank now had names, but he also had another clue. Lying in the evidence box was the bloody mariner's cap. In Seattle, Cruickshank watched yet another retail clerk flick through receipts, and this clerk said he remembered a man who bought a cap. The customer had admitted he was running booze from Canada. Cruickshank showed some photos to the clerk, who pointed to one. The name on the back of the photo was Owen Benjamin Baker.

Cruickshank and Sergeant Bob Owens followed up other leads. A small-time bootlegger cooling his heels in the Anacortes jail said the green-painted sack came from Baker. A Victoria boatyard owner said a customer wanted the upper structure on an old boat changed, but gave no reason. The boater's name was Stromkins. On Pender Island, the liquor-bagging farmer took one glance at one of Owens's photos and said, "Why there's Paul, Paul Stromkins." Eventually, and only because clever BCPP officers managed

Inspector Forbes Cruickshank of the BCPP became a hero after he solved the mystery of the *Beryl G* disappearances and brought three murderous hijackers to justice.

to snare him in a lie, Stromkins fingered Morris, Sowash and Baker. Yes, he was there during the killings, Stromkins stammered, but he never set foot on *Beryl G*; he was in a dinghy, busy rowing liquor ashore.

Seattle police found Morris in the city, where he fought against extradition. Sowash was arrested in New Orleans and wrote a confession implicating Baker and Morris. Baker was handcuffed in New York City. By June 1925, Baker and Sowash were fighting for their lives in a Victoria courtroom during a week-long murder trial that captured the imagination of the public on both sides of the border. The jury heard the charge against Paul Stromkins read aloud and watched the prosecutor rise to his feet. There were audible gasps when Archibald Johnson told the judge, "The prosecution has no evidence to offer against the accused." Stromkins was a free man. Then it was learned Baker's former accomplice would be the Crown's key witness. Surprise followed surprise: Baker and Sowash had opted to defend themselves.

For many crowding onto the pew-like wooden benches arrayed before the raised magistrate's bench, the legal drama represented nothing more than titillating entertainment. For bootlegger Pete Marinoff, squeezed in with the rest, courtroom events represented something much more important—an opportunity to get some deep personal satisfaction. Watching Crown Prosecutor Archibald Johnson win guilty verdicts against the murderous *Beryl G* hijackers was just part of it.

Some of Marinoff's bitterness was rooted in a particularly galling episode that had occurred years earlier. Rolling a car loaded with whisky through Tacoma, Marinoff had been tricked into stopping by two highway hijackers posing as police. The two absconded with 14 cases of liquor. Adding insult to injury, one hijacker had extracted all the money from Marinoff's wallet and then, in a move that had members of Marinoff's bootlegging fraternity shaking with laughter, had handcuffed Pete and his driver to their car. The fact that this hijacker was later convicted of the theft of $100 and did a three-year stretch behind bars hardly salved Marinoff's wounded pride. The hijacker who had made Pete a laughingstock was none other than the smirking, thickset individual sitting in the prisoner's dock—"Cannonball" Baker. The decision of the accused to represent themselves in court afforded Pete Marinoff the opportunity, while under cross-examination by Baker, to remind the former highway hijacker of the earlier roadside holdup, much to the amusement of Crown Prosecutor Archibald Johnson, the fascination of jury members and the delight of spectators.

The trial's climactic moment came when Paul Stromkins was called to testify. The trembling man began to tell his story. His agitation increased as he related the terrible moment when, sitting in a dingy, he heard two shots from inside *Beryl G.*

"You must tell the court what you saw, Mr. Stromkins," Archie Johnson urged him quietly. "All of it."

"I saw young Gillis come on deck with Sowash behind him. Then, Harry's hand went up and he brought something crashing down on the boy's head." Gasping and quaking, Stromkins continued the tale. "Morris and Baker came up from the cabin . . . they were carrying Captain Gillis. He was dead." Stromkins's hands gripped the sides of the witness box, and his voice became shrill. "They were both dead . . . Gillis and his son . . . both of them." Stromkins covered his face with his hands and wept. Then he provided a fitting climax for the drama, reliving the horrific moment when the two bodies were wrapped in the boat's anchor chain. "Oh, my God!" Stromkins blurted. "Baker slashed the bodies with his knife so they would sink more quickly!"

The day the judge passed sentence—Sowash and Baker would "hang by the neck" until dead—Charlie Morris was crossing the border, extradited at last. Once again, Stromkins testified that Morris was in the dingy with him and had no part in the actual murder. It didn't matter; Morris was found guilty, and the judge ordered the death penalty. Morris appealed and his sentence was commuted to life behind bars. Stromkins walked free, while Inspector Forbes Cruickshank basked in well-deserved recognition as a latter-day BC Sherlock Holmes.

The wholesale price of liquor inside the hold of *Beryl G* was just $20 a case, but its actual cost was much, much higher than even the 200-dollar-a-case retail value. It had come at the steepest price imaginable: the lives of four men.

But what of the Eggers brothers and their infamous *M-197*? Not long after the trio sold their boat to another rum-runner, it also became a hijacking victim. After a few ill-fated runs, the disabled craft was towed from wharf to deep water by Roy Olmstead's men, who sank her without ceremony. Quite soon, the Eggers brothers' fortunes began to founder, as well. By early November 1924, the long arm of Canadian law had reached down to San Francisco, grabbed Micky and Happy and, through extradition, had begun to pull the two up to BC to face piracy charges. Brother Ted and his associates attempted to snatch them back. In an audacious daylight attack on a busy staircase of the Bay City's federal building, they sprayed ammonia in the face of a deputy marshal, sending him reeling. That still wasn't good enough for one member of the gang, who took a shot at the agonized guard. The bullet missed him but instead buried itself in Happy's chest. The group hustled Micky out of the building and into a waiting car, leaving Happy to die.

Now the San Francisco cops wanted Ted for attempted murder of the deputy marshal. Privately, they felt the shooter had done everyone a favour by inadvertently killing Ted's brother. Six months later, Ted was arrested in Seattle and hustled north for trial. When witnesses couldn't identify him, he was returned to Seattle, where he was sentenced to six months behind bars for Micky's escape.

It took two years before police brought Micky to Victoria aboard Coast Guard cutter *Arcata*. In court, Eggers was told he would be bound over for trial in the fall. The tough guy burst into tears. Things immediately went from unseemly to bizarre as his next of kin—wife, sister, mother and father—all began wailing and shouting. After months in Oakalla, Micky Eggers was in court again.

"Is the man you saw on the *Kayak* in this courtroom?" the Crown attorney asked previously cooperative deck-hand Troy Martin. He had told the Crown that he had seen Micky's face as he briefly pulled down his mask. Now, with Micky's family looking on, Martin hedged. "Well I couldn't say definitely," he mumbled. Testimony by family members provided Micky's rock-solid alibi. The jury took less than half an hour to find him not guilty.

Micky's freedom ended a few days later. He was arrested by Seattle police, along with six others, after a botched robbery of the Baghdad Theatre. Included in the dragnet was a woman a suspicious policeman had seen in the getaway car outside the theatre—Micky's wife, Dorothy. The jury found Micky guilty. The last of the notorious pirate trio was jailed as just another failed stickup artist.

10

The Good Bootlegger

SEATTLE BOOTLEG DRIVER CLIFF SMITH was angry. It was supposed to be just another run and should have gone off smoothly. Instead, out of nowhere, a motorcycle cop had waved their truck over to the curb. The cop acted like he didn't have a clue and then proved it by impounding the truck and confiscating the load.

As soon as the cops allowed him, Smith called his boss.

"What's wrong?" Roy Olmstead asked, rubbing sleep from his eyes.

"A two-wheeler got us," Smith shouted.

"Who?" Olmstead asked.

"Don't know. Got a funny name," Smith snarled.

Olmstead might have been upset by Smith's tone, but by

the summer of 1924, Seattle's number-one bootlegger had far bigger worries than a surly underling. "Did you have a load on?" he asked.

"Yes," Smith answered curtly. What a stupid question! Of course he had a load. Police pulling over an empty truck was something you and the boss chuckled about later over drinks. But a truck carrying crates of whisky stacked to the top of the canvas covering was something else again.

"I'll take care of it right away," Olmstead told Smith.

Olmstead was worried. It seemed the police were out to get him. But why? Wasn't he paying the boys in blue plenty to keep them onside? Certain officers got their cash on the tenth of every month, as regular as clockwork. More look-the-other-way money went to King County sheriff's deputies and harbour-patrol personnel.

Unbeknownst to Olmstead, Police Chief Bill Severyns had whined to Mayor Edwin "Doc" Brown about Olmstead's liquor-ring operations. By now, the public was calling the kingpin of Western Freighters—now one of the city's biggest employers—"the good bootlegger." True, 30 Seattle residents died every year and dozens more suffered temporary blindness or paralysis from drinking potentially deadly moonshine, but just because Olmstead peddled high-quality commercially produced liquor wasn't reason enough to allow him to build a virtual liquor monopoly. Allow a man to get too big and he got dangerous.

Like Doc, Severyns was supposedly an Olmstead

"friendly" and had briefly paid the price. While Doc was in New York, acting-mayor Bertha Landes had declared a state of emergency, fired Severyns and appointed herself police chief. That got the mayor scuttling back to the West Coast in a hurry. He got Severyns back into the chief's uniform, much to the liquor-ring's relief, but that relief would be short-lived. Face-saving Doc gave his chief the nod, and Severyns passed the word down: Hit Olmstead's trucks! Hit Olmstead's plants!

Minutes after his conversation with Smith, Olmstead managed to reach the "two-wheeler," a patrolman named Baerman. "I understand that you picked up one of my boys," Olmstead began patiently.

"Yes. It was too raw [obvious]," Baerman answered apologetically. "He was loaded to the axles. I've passed up your boys several times before, but this was too raw."

At this time of night, Olmstead didn't have the patience to dance around. "Whaddya want?" he asked.

"It's not up to me," Baerman replied peevishly. He had a couple of questions of his own: "What do *you* want to do? What have you been doing for the motorcycle boys?" Baerman already knew the answer to that one.

"I haven't been doing anything," Olmstead admitted, and then got a little peevish himself. "Jesus Christ, it's split up four ways now, and when I get through I have nothing left!"

Olmstead could hear the shrug in Baerman's voice, "Well, it's up to you."

"No, it's not up to me. It's up to you," Olmstead snapped.

Okay, Baerman decided, Smith could spend a night in the clink. "I'm going to turn him in," the policeman told Olmstead. Then, he twisted the knife, "I have an idea there is going to be a change soon."

Roy Olmstead had heard enough. "All right, do as you damn please about it!" He slammed the receiver down into the bracket, breaking the connection.

Patrolman Baerman stared at the silent phone. It's up to you, Roy had said. Baerman cursed himself for being a hothead; Olmstead's phrase was code for "name your price."

The phone on Olmstead's bedside table jangled. It was Baerman. "I don't want to seem unreasonable, Roy, but I thought you were trying to lord it over me."

Olmstead stifled a sigh. "No, I've been asleep and I haven't got my eyes open yet." Then a cautionary thought crawled through his sleep-fogged brain. "Be careful what you say. My line is tapped."

"Well, I think it ought to be worth a century, Roy," Baerman replied softly.

A measly hundred bucks to spring Smith and recover the liquor! Olmstead smiled. This guy was definitely doomed to straddle a motorcycle until retirement. "Well why didn't you say so before?" the bootlegger told the cop. "All right, come on over to the house and we'll talk it over."

Roy Olmstead was right: others were listening in. An electronic innovation called wire-tapping allowed federal

Prohibition agents to hear conversations as clearly as if they had been sitting in on Olmstead's meetings with liquor-ring partners, plant managers, dispatchers, liquor suppliers, delivery men, on-the-take policemen—including the department's dry-squad leader—and various fixers, including a notable customs broker.

If the feds couldn't get to Olmstead any other way, they hoped conversations scribbled by agents clutching phone receivers to their ears would do the trick. William Whitney's wife, Clara, a professional stenographer, typed up the dialogues. Roy Olmstead professed unconcern, since wiretapped conversations were inadmissible as courtroom evidence. Still, while on the telephone, code names replaced real names on the "Commander's" orders. In spite of these precautions, eavesdropping agents soon heard reassuring confirmation that shore-patrol and Coast Guard efforts, not to mention hijackers' raids, were seriously hurting Olmstead's organization.

"Take down these numbers: 90, 256, 51 [cases of liquor apprehended or stolen]—that's what we lost. How's it going to be figured?" an Olmstead money man asked.

"I'll call you afterward about that," Olmstead replied.

"What I want to know, does Bennie Goldsmith [a liquor-ring partner and major West Coast bootlegger] and his crowd stand half the loss?"

"About the loss—it's absorbed 50 percent by Fleming [political fixer and liquor distributor] and others."

"Then 25 percent is absorbed by us?"

"Yes."

There were a few moments of silence while swift calculations were completed.

"That's a $9,000 loss; our share is only $798.13!"

"Yes, that's about right. Sales last month ran $176,000; freight was $18,000, and the stuff cost us $154,000. It's a big loss—awful."

By fall, Olmstead's life got tougher. Off Portland Island, BC, a Canadian customs boat surprised his *Eva B* in the middle of a liquor transfer. Olmstead went to Victoria and bailed out the crew, but couldn't retrieve *Eva B*, later sold for $40,000 to satisfy the smuggling fine and costs. Its cargo—an estimated 60 cases of ordinary Scotch whisky and another 64 cases of expensive Pebbleford bourbon—remained beyond his grasp. It was a major blow; the ring's typical profit from just 100 cases was as much as a federal Prohibition agent's annual salary.

One night in the blustery fall of 1924, Whitney and his wife, posing as Roy Olmstead and his wife, Elsie, called some of the ring's fetch-and-carry men and told them to come quickly to Olmstead's comfortable two-storey home. The arriving men were arrested at the corner address as soon as they stepped out of their cars. After a 2 AM ham-and-egg breakfast prepared by the Olmstead cook, nine men and three women, including Roy and his wife, were driven "downtown." Predictably, the Olmsteads' lawyer, George Vanderveer, quickly arranged bail. However, the wheels of justice were rolling inexorably toward a trial. When that trial took place in January 1926, the *Seattle Daily Times* exclaimed, "WHISPERING WIRES TELL MORE!"

Defence lawyer George Vanderveer attempted to turn a bootlegging-ring trial into a government conspiracy-to-eavesdrop trial. However, with some limitations on its use—testifying agents had to memorize conversations, rather than read them—a 775-page wiretap book was entered into evidence, thus setting a legal precedent. The testimony of two of the 125 witnesses, dispatcher John McLean and Ed Hutmaker, the elderly caretaker of the Viele Ranch, Olmstead's rural storage depot, sealed the fate of Olmstead and 20 others. On the stand, Hutmaker stated that Fourth of July business was so frantic, Olmstead himself made the 45-minute drive to the ranch to supervise and assist truck loading. It was a decision that cost Olmstead dearly. He was found guilty of conspiracy to import and/or conspiracy to transport and deliver. His punishment was two years in prison, two years of hard labour and a fine of $1.6 million.

The feds weren't through with Olmstead's associates. That spring, 40 defendants were indicted in a second case. Olmstead's chief lieutenant, Alfred Hubbard, was star prosecution witness. The jury convicted all of the rum-runners—but none of the indicted who held public office. Minutes later, the wife of rum-runner Bennie Goldsmith dashed into the courthouse and socked turncoat Hubbard on the jaw. Whitney raced up, revolver drawn, screaming "Peace, in the name of the United States!"

Pete Marinoff was undoubtedly delighted with the fall of a major competitor. Marinoff bootlegged liquor until US Prohibition's repeal. Someone else also breathed a sigh of relief: rum-runner Johnny Schnarr. Olmstead's Robin Hood–like aura wasn't surprising. Literally thousands of Seattle and Puget Sound residents owed the man their livelihoods. But Johnny Schnarr claimed that Olmstead owed him money. Three of Johnny's Olmstead loads went unpaid; Olmstead's contact men gave various excuses for not having the money ready. When Olmstead's boys called Johnny up for a fourth run, Schnarr told Consolidated he wasn't going to haul for Olmstead again until he was paid. Olmstead promised the money, but Johnny wouldn't budge. "They moaned and groaned a lot, but I finally got my way and the money was sent." That fourth trip was the last he made for Olmstead. "It just wasn't worth the trouble," Johnny later explained. "I never lost a cent . . . but a lot of other people never got paid." Before his arrest, Consolidated Exporters had cut Olmstead off, too. The rumour was he owed Consolidated $280,000.

Behind bars, Olmstead saw the error of his ways and became a Christian Scientist, receiving a presidential pardon in 1935. By 1940, he was returning regularly to McNeil Island, this time to provide spiritual guidance to inmates. Was he Roy Olmstead, the bootlegger? inmates asked. "No," Roy replied. "That person no longer exists."

11

Out of "Control"

PROHIBITION MAY HAVE BEEN REPEALED in BC, but if John Q. Public thought buying alcohol would be as simple as walking into a government store, he had a shock coming. While the booze itself was usually better quality than what most bootleggers had offered, it was actually more difficult to buy a bottle under liquor control than during prohibition. Voters who had banished prohibition in favour of liquor control expected government officials—who had never run a business—to organize and run a complex enterprise complete with purchasing, warehousing and province-wide shipping and retailing within four months of the passage of the Government Liquor Act. They managed it, but their efforts would bedevil the province for generations to come.

Before setting foot inside a liquor store, a thirsty person was required to visit the nearest BCPP office to purchase something no bootlegger demanded: a permit costing as much as five dollars—a day's pay for many. Bootleggers didn't care what or how much your first order was, but the government did. A first-purchase limit was a dozen beer. A midnight thirst once meant a fast call to an obliging bootlegger. By government decree, liquor stores closed by 8 PM As a result, bootlegging continued to flourish.

A bootleg purchase was usually a simple, enjoyable experience. Government store personnel acted as if they were entrusting purchasers with a hazardous substance. Once inside the dark, drab and cheerless liquor stores, customers couldn't even touch a bottle before buying. Purchasers stood in front of a forbidding counter; the clerks stood behind it. One employee examined the permit in question and stamped it. Another took the order—the customer pointed to or verbalized his or her request—and wrote it down. The order slip was then handed to a third clerk who removed the selected bottle from the shelf and placed it in a brown paper bag. Money changed hands, and the package was handed to the customer. However, liquor-store business boomed, thanks, in part, to liquor-deprived Americans. That summer, an estimated 75 percent of Vancouver stores' business came from American tourists, who dropped $20,000 on the Fourth of July weekend alone. BC drinkers soon had an alternative to what wags called

"John Oliver Drugstores": tax-exempt importers, who seriously undercut the BC government prices—no five-dollar permit required. Nine months after the first BC Liquor Control Board (LCB) stores opened, thirsty, thrifty British Columbians had imported over 360,000 gallons of beer and nearly 60,000 gallons of spirits and wine.

New liquor regulations were both draconian and absurd. An apprehended inebriate immediately forfeited his coveted permit, while drunkenness was prohibited in the privacy of one's own home—or in a car or boat or aboard a train. LCB inspectors could search any of them without warrants. While potential drinkers were perplexed, amused and frustrated by the new system, the municipalities in which they lived loved it; the provincial government offered them half the profits of liquor sales. A three-member Liquor Control Board ran things under the direction of the Attorney General. Only the provincial Cabinet could alter the triumvirate's decisions, which placed it above the judicial system.

The men working behind store counters, inside warehouses and undertaking investigations were a fortunate few of the 5,000 who applied for LCB positions. Most weren't chosen because of any special knowledge, wartime service or exemplary employment history. The professional background of LCB chief inspector George Miller raised some eyebrows. During prohibition, Miller was employed by Vancouver's Strand Hotel as head waiter at the time of a successful dry-squad raid. Later, he worked for disgraced Prohibition Commissioner Findlay. Miller's assistant, Chief Detective David Scott, also had a questionable background. While a Vancouver city cop, Scott had been investigated by the department on unspecified charges of "a serious nature" and summarily dismissed. These men and many others landed their new jobs through Liberal party connections. Premier Harlan Brewster had promised to end patronage, but by 1921, that promise was as dead as the man who made it.

Conservative Billy Bowser, now opposition leader, understood patronage plums very well. He described the LCB as a "partisan, supine Commission," and reminded backbenchers that "the government is controlled by the Attorney General, the wicked partner of the Premier." Bowser was pointing his accusatory finger at Attorney General J.W. Farris, who soon resigned after revelations of a corruption-tainted liquor warehouse contract. The LCB had taken out an option to purchase a warehouse for $150,000, despite its city assessment of just $58,000. The warehouse was owned by Charles Campbell, a prominent Liberal and a Farris friend.

The new LCB boss, Attorney General Alexander Manson, disliked the liquor industry intensely. That made Reverend A.E. Cooke, spokesman for the new BC Prohibition Association, hopeful. "I am doing my utmost through our Vendors to see that the amount of liquor consumed by the individual is curtailed," Manson told Cooke, "so that the least possible harm can come to the individual drinker and his family from the use of liquor."

Those who made the LCB run did not share Manson's morals-before-money philosophy. Eager to market to thirsty American tourists disembarking from steamships, board executives decided to locate Victoria's second liquor outlet near the inner harbour. Hunching the Attorney General would scuttle the plan, the executives went over his head and asked the premier himself to personally inspect the proposed site. Premier Oliver did so and gave the board his approval. When Manson heard the news, he quickly announced there would be no second store in Victoria anywhere and sternly reminded board employees (and those who read the *Victoria Daily Times'* story) that the LCB was put into place to control liquor consumption, not to increase it.

Patronage almost guaranteed mismanagement. Many LCB employees were incompetent, and some couldn't even manage to cover their unethical tracks. A $5,000 discrepancy between stock and entries at the Hastings Street liquor store resulted in the entire staff of 15—both the guilty and the innocent—being tossed out on their ears. Soon afterward, the same discrepancy was discovered at Beatty Street and Pender Street stores. During a Manson crackdown, the Dominion Liquor Company was charged with illegal sales, likely to bootleggers. As its defence lawyer, Dominion hired none other than J.W. Farris, who had resumed his legal career after resigning as Attorney General.

Not all LCB personnel were cosy cronies. Infighting—especially between Chairman A.M. Johnson and Commissioner J.H. Falconer—was vicious. Falconer rarely went to Victoria; a key player in the Vancouver Liberal machine, the rogue commissioner acted independently, rewarding special mainland friends, including licence-granting William McArthur. "Get it clearly into your head once and for all that you are not the Board," Manson wrote Falconer bluntly. "In no sense are you in charge of the Vancouver Warehouse or the Vancouver Stores. You are a member of a Board of Three." Falconer was far too busy filling his increasingly heavy pocket to listen to Manson. A paid informant tipped the Attorney General that Falconer had accepted $15,000 from the British Columbia Distillery Company, keeping $5,000 for himself. It took two years, but Falconer was finally forced to resign.

In the wake of major public scandals and a host of other warehouse and store shenanigans, some British Columbians may have wondered whether outright prohibition was all that bad. Americans would have set them straight. Beyond the big-city liquor lawlessness of Seattle and Portland, where, the *Oregonian* confessed, a home-brew frenzy meant Prohibition enforcement was "impracticable and impossible," booze had become a deadly business.

In the mountains southeast of Spokane, deputy sheriffs signalled known bootlegger Arthur Jahns to stop his car. When he didn't, a lawman fired his shotgun, intending to

Using US Prohibition as much to promote himself as to bring bootleggers to justice, King County sheriff Matt Starwich smashes bottles of confiscated liquor for the camera. UNIVERSITY OF WASHINGTON SPECIAL DOLLECTIONS, PH COLL 676.10, PROHIBITION ERA/MATT STARWICH COLLECTION, UW11447

puncture Jahns's tire but fatally puncturing the bootlegger instead. In Skamania County, federal agent James Morgan and Clark County deputy sheriff W.E. Rorison surprised Paul Hickey and Harold Ahola at work at their still. "Surrender!" the lawmen yelled. While Ahola dashed away, Hickey let loose with his 30-30, hitting both Rorison and Morgan. Agent Morgan kept shooting, so Hickey shot him again—in the head. The dying Rorison managed to get off one last shot, killing Hickey.

Five years later, in 1927, the same county suffered another casualty. As the *Oregonian* put it, recently elected county sheriff Lester Wood had begun his term by "conducting a ruthless war on liquor violators." When three of Wood's deputies discovered a 125-gallon still operation at an abandoned logging camp 25 miles northeast of Vancouver, Washington, they were apprehended by bootlegger Ellis Baker and marched at gunpoint back down the trail. Reaching the nearest telephone, the lawmen called for backup. Wood and another deputy drove out from Vancouver.

While one deputy waited for Wood, his two companions returned to the apparently deserted site, determined to destroy the still. Anticipating the lawmen would reappear, Ellis and his brother Luther were crouched in the bush. However, seconds away from ambushing the two deputies, they were surprised by Wood and the others. Aiming his shotgun, Wood yelled, "Put up your hands, I'm the sheriff!" Luther put up his rifle instead and blasted Wood in the hip. Dodging bullets, the Bakers made their escape. Minutes later, Wood was dead. After a headline-making murder trial, Luther died for his crime at the hands of the hangman. For his part in Wood's death, Ellis Baker would spend 30 years behind bars in Walla Walla's state penitentiary.

There were no liquor-related police fatalities in BC, and the worst fate that could befall provincial liquor violators was six months of hard labour. Perhaps West Coast Canadians were different after all.

CHAPTER

12

BC's Beer Blues

VANCOUVER HOTEL OPERATOR H.J. McSorley was excited. Renovations to the Palace, undertaken to meet government liquor-control specifications, had set him and his partner back thousands of dollars, but none of that would matter with a beer-parlour licence hanging on the wall. Forget the rooms upstairs! Thanks to BC's 1925 beer-by-the-glass legislation, it was the parlour downstairs that would boost the Palace's profits. Once their loans were paid off, they'd be strolling down easy street.

Weeks later, with easy street nowhere in sight, McSorley confronted LCB "big cheese" William T. McArthur, asking why his licence application had been denied. McSorley played his trump card: if he didn't get that parlour licence damn quick, he would tell his story directly to the LCB boss, Attorney General Alex Manson.

"What pull do you think you have to get a licence over me?" McArthur asked.

"The promises of four cabinet ministers," the would-be parlour operator boasted.

"I don't give a [expletive] for all the cabinet ministers in Victoria," McArthur sneered. "I'm running Vancouver and will see who gets licences."

LCB squabbles and scandals were but a prelude to the biggest battle of BC's 1920s liquor wars: public drinking. The Liberal government vowed the saloon would never return, crafting an Act that banned words associated with the era, including "bar," "bar-room," "saloon," "tavern" and "cocktail." Even decades later, BC visitors strolling American streets took delight in the novel sight of neon signs flashing those still-forbidden words.

Veterans, brewers and hotel owners wanted legalized public beer drinking, which, advocates argued, would deliver a knockout blow to bootlegging. Vancouver Liberal MLA Ian Mackenzie and Fernie independent MLA Tom Uphill (representing a riding that was home to some of BC's most notorious rum-runners) wanted public drinking, too. A working-man's champion, Uphill saw the legislation as discriminatory, claiming that the cars of affluent residents allowed them to transport beer to their private beer cellars while "the poor man has neither" cars nor beer cellars.

Former soldiers were publicly quaffing beer and booze anyway. Veterans' clubs allowed members who had fought and survived the First World War to celebrate that fact, and anything else they chose to celebrate, with either the club's beer or hard liquor carried into the premises. When the LCB refused to supply beer to clubs, operators simply gave the board a private address and then had the suds rerouted to the club. It didn't take long for hotels to want a piece of the new beer action. Close to 50 hotels applied for club status.

The government feared that enforcing prohibition at clubs would enrage tens of thousands of veterans who would carry that anger into polling booths. The *Vancouver Province* challenged the vacillating Attorney General on the issue. The resulting front-page story indicated that Farris had allowed the clubs to serve beer after all, rendering the law meaningless. Stung by the backlash, Farris sicced government "booze hounds" on the clubs. Dozens of club charters were revoked. Constables accompanied all beer deliveries to ensure they were bound for legitimate destinations. Close to 700 liquor charges clogged Vancouver's courtrooms. To the government's embarrassment, many cases were thrown out. Judges ruled that a club was not a person and therefore could not be prosecuted. When some confiscated bottles of beer had no appropriate government seal, Judge H.S. Caley ruled that whatever was in those bottles, it couldn't be liquor. Case dismissed. Caley dismissed another case because the common practice of charging club members a service fee for distributing beer that members had carried in and stored in lockers was not, strictly speaking, "selling" beer.

The Attorney General's strategists pondered the club dilemma and by 1924 had found a solution. Any organization or business could apply for a new $100 LCB club licence allowing them to sell beer. The government saved face and pocketed a tidy profit, not only on increased beer sales, but on fees from club licences.

This didn't help beleaguered hotel owners. During the post-war recession, hotel taxes had risen while revenues had fallen; many hotels were operating at less than 50 percent capacity. Moreover, the Liquor Act allowed guests to drink liquor privately in their rooms, which some boozers turned into disgusting drinking dens. One Fernie hotelier complained that his best rooms featured dirty carpets, chipped plaster and walls "stained by vomit as high up as six feet."

The labour movement and general public were divided on the issue, and the Liberals likely hoped that more compelling issues would overshadow the beer plebiscite. Vote-hungry 1924 election candidates predictably dodged the thorny beer issue or attempted to ignore it. Not even the newly formed Canadian Labour Party took an official plebiscite stand. "A mere detail," sniffed *BC Federationist* editors; the real issue in BC was jobs. Legal public drinking would lower unemployment. The image of construction crews erecting new breweries to augment the few that had managed to survive prohibition was just one of several exciting fantasies. Just imagine—there could be thousands of workers streaming into those new facilities to produce beer 24/7, in addition to new beer clubs desperate for hundreds of waiters, understaffed cooperages hiring more men to manufacture beer barrels, and cartage companies recruiting more drivers to deliver the beer to all those new hotel drinking establishments. So, despite a divided government and perhaps because of a divided opposition, the legislature finally passed a plebiscite bill.

The ballot asked, "Do you approve of the sale of beer by the glass in licensed premises without a bar under Government control and regulation?" The phrase "without a bar" was no idle afterthought. Its inclusion was meant to reassure voters that a plebiscite victory did not mean a return to disreputable saloons. The public was not reassured. Beer by the glass went down to defeat, 73,853 votes to 72,214. Many voters apparently questioned the government's ability to regulate expanded public drinking when it hadn't effectively enforced control over, or even run, the LCB in an ethical way. "Recount!" cried moderationists. "Victory!" shouted prohibitionists.

The Liquor Act stipulated that those residing in "yes" ridings could apply for beer licences and that meant residents of over half of the province's electoral districts, including Vancouver, Burnaby and Fernie, where 78 percent voted in favour. The *Vancouver Sun* shouted, "BEER BY THE GLASS NOT DEAD," while non-plussed, dry-leaning Attorney

General Manson appeared to contradict the Liquor Act, saying, "whether those places which voted for [beer by the glass] should be granted the privilege . . . has yet to be decided." In the 23 ridings that had voted "yes," what was there left to decide?

Meanwhile, results of other balloting revealed that voters doubted the Liberal's ability to tackle any issue, liquor or otherwise. John Oliver now led a minority government and desperately needed the support of independent MLAs, including Fernie's victorious incumbent Tom Uphill, who was fast losing patience. "If Vancouver wants to drink fizz, all right," Uphill told the *Vancouver Province*, "but my constituents voted four to one for beer and I want to see something done and done quickly." The final vote came in December. Oliver himself—tears of remorse coursing down his cheeks—finally cast his personal vote for beer, as the government and opposition MLAs legalized beer by the glass.

Understandings and gentlemen's agreements between the government and the new BC Hotel Association (BCHA) limited the "free enterprise" beer-by-the-glass business to hotel owners and over a dozen veterans' groups amalgamated a year later as the new Canadian Legion. Any number of reasons could doom a licence application, including the wrong party affiliation, as H.J. McSorley discovered. The Liberal-supporting operator of the Astoria was soon displaying the licence that Conservative McSorley felt should have been hanging in the Palace. Any individual entrepreneur who wished to establish a free-standing beer parlour was denied. There would be no return to the saloon. The rule was "hotel first, then beer licence—maybe." The "beer parlours" that hoteliers soon created in strict accord with government regulations would not change for three generations.

Operational rules were quickly hammered into place. With one exception, these increasingly anachronistic regulations defied all efforts to pry them loose. Decades of patrons could be forgiven for thinking that while eagerly calculating licence revenues, LCB civil servants had contrived to punish those engaged in a distasteful vice by forcing them to empty their glasses in the most dismal environments conceivable. As big-band swing morphed into psychedelic feedback and the wide-eyed wackiness of *I Love Lucy* became the sly Vietnam commentary of *M*A*S*H*, BC beer-parlour ambience remained a testament to 19th-century saloon abhorrence. There were no jukeboxes or TVs; patrons who wanted to hear music or watch TV were forced to leave the parlour. Hunger also drove them out; food was forbidden, as were games. No cards—for either high-stakes poker or lowly bridge—were allowed at tables. Beer drinkers couldn't admire photos or paintings, be they Betty Grable pinups or Elvis velvet paintings. Patrons simply sat, smoked and drank. The only alcoholic beverage allowed was a glass of beer.

However, the new establishments made one concession that former saloons did not: they permitted female customers.

In a rare enlightened decision, the provincial government decided that banning women, as the LCB chairman put it, "appeared unreasonable and ungallant to the fair sex." Talk was cheap when most women understandably avoided the vapid places. Many men did, too, including thousands of immigrants from old Blighty who fondly remembered the warm hospitality found inside British pubs, where happy, guilt-free patrons enjoyed impromptu singalongs and games of darts. Others, feeling the subtle pressure of male bonding, walked in forcing smiles to hide their secret "hold-your-nose" reluctance. Holding one's nose threatened to become more than a turn of phrase, as gasping arrivals penetrated a wall of warm, smoke-laden air redolent of stale beer and sweat. Decades later, the experience remained unchanged.

Beer parlours spread alarmingly fast. A few months after legalization, there were over 60 in Vancouver alone. A Vancouver anti-beer league quickly raised $10,000 to finance efforts to force another province-wide beer plebiscite based on the notion that parlours were a threat to families. Mistaking women for "families," misguided BCHA members concluded that banning women from their parlours would mollify the agitators. The hotel owners' second reason for considering a ban on women had more substance. Many patrons resented the mere possibility of women being allowed in their exclusively male enclave, one of the very few places they could truly be themselves, a sentiment they shared with the saloon patrons of yesteryear.

However, the Attorney General advised there was no legal way to prohibit women from stepping inside. Instead, in a legally questionable move, the LCB posted signs warning women to stay away. Both the *Vancouver Sun* and *Province* approved the move. "There are plenty of sound reasons for keeping women out of beer parlours frequented by men," the *Sun* reminded readers, without defining what those sound reasons were.

The *Province*, in the delicate phrasing of the day, hinted more broadly, "There is no doubt that the presence of women makes it more difficult to conduct beer parlours in a decent and orderly manner." Why? Were wives and mothers noisier than husbands and fathers? Did they act more violently? Were women even more unable than men to hold their liquor? Astute newspaper readers knew the real reason for the anti-female bias. The females in question were prostitutes, ready and willing to corrupt and sicken their husbands, brothers and sons. After all, given the parlours' environment and purpose, what other kind of woman would willingly step inside? Having a husband return home drunk to wife and family was bad; having him stagger through the door infected with a sexually transmitted disease was worse. Once again, BC's modern 20th-century society was attempting to come to grips with an old 19th-century saloon-era fear—and doing it badly.

The BC Prohibition Association also might have been expected to applaud the ban, but surprisingly, the association's Reverend R.J. McIntyre—without using the terminology that would become common 50 years later—saw it as a violation of gender equality. However, he revealed his true motive by advising the government that, "If beer parlours were unfit for decent women, then remove the parlours, not the women."

What to do? It took an individual hotel operator, Albert Lake, to answer the question. When women showed up at his Commercial Hotel for beer, Lake directed them to a separate room. That stopped complaints cold. To the enormous relief of the BCHA, the prohibitionists' plebiscite was avoided. As time went on, some hotel operators became very clever in avoiding the potentially volatile mix of men, women and beer. In the early 1960s, Victoria's Victor Ingraham installed an ingenious retractable wall set on wheels in the Ingraham Hotel's 500-seat parlour. When one side of the Ingy's beer parlour filled with thirsty customers, two waiters would wheel the wall to the emptier female side allowing for more space for patrons. While the separate-room, separate-entrance decision allayed public animosity, it only reinforced the notion that beer parlours were disreputable places that no well-balanced, healthy person would willingly patronize. Today, pedestrians still walk beneath three peculiar, barely visible words above certain hotel doorways. First etched into stone and concrete almost a century ago are the words "Ladies and Escorts."

Prohibition's Shadow

ARDENT ANTI-SALOON LEAGUE MEMBER Delcevare King was angry. Millions were guzzling illegal booze and threatening Prohibition's promise of a sane, sober America. King figured the lawbreakers should be given a name "which best expresses the idea of lawless drinker . . . with the biting power of 'scab' or 'slacker.'" King announced a contest, offering $200 for the best "rum-word" submitted. "Contestants pour in words to fit the man who drinks," reported the *Boston Herald*. The 25,000 entries included slime-slopper, stillwhacker, rum-rough, and lawlessite. Henry Irving Dale and Miss Kate L. Butler both submitted the identical winning term: scofflaw. The *New York Times* hoped the label would give bootleg patrons "the pain they deserve." Instead, boozers considered "scofflaw" a badge of honour. A *New York Post* reader best captured the public's mood:

> I want to be a scofflaw
> And with the scofflaws stand;
> A brand upon my forehead
> A handcuff on my hand.

When liquor laws became laughable, US Prohibition was doomed. It was finally repealed in 1933, as BC's prohibition had been 13 years earlier.

Governments are slow to change liquor regulations, and this intransigence is magnified when two levels of government are involved. Canadian Native prohibition was both a federal and provincial issue. The process of change moved as slowly on Ottawa's Parliament Hill as it did inside Victoria's Legislative Buildings. It didn't help that the BC government was often contemptuous of the federal government. In response to federal Indian Act changes, BC finally allowed Natives to drink publicly in beer parlours, but not in veterans' clubs.

Native people were divided on the drinking issue. Native war veterans felt they had earned the right to drink anywhere they chose. The liquor issue became a larger one about equality. Admitted one 1950s coastal Native, "When I get drunk I keep thinking about all the crooked things the white people have done to us, and I keep getting madder and madder and pretty soon I am ready to fight."

One August night in 1958 in Prince Rupert, the BC city with the largest Native population at the time, RCMP officers attempted to arrest two Native street brawlers. Emerging from beer parlours after last call, white and Native patrons joined the fracas. Before long, police faced a rock-and-bottle-tossing mob of a thousand. Mayor Peter Lester read the Riot Act twice, and police lobbed 25 canisters of tear gas into the throng. Dozens were jailed; 39—including 24 Natives—were charged with various crimes.

Many factors helped spark the violence, but Mayor Lester focused on liquor complaints. "Indians can only drink in beer parlours and not [even] in their homes. They don't like it," he told reporters. City council quickly passed a resolution calling for Aboriginal liquor equality. At the Native Brotherhood's annual meeting, delegates overwhelmingly passed a resolution for full liquor rights. Federal–provincial government buck-passing (BC Attorney General Robert Bonner blamed the Indian Act for creating a "fantastic rigmarole") and Native issues, from on-reserve drinking to band autonomy, slowed progress. It wasn't until July 1962 that the government extended full liquor privileges to all BC First Nations people. Forty-four bands out of 47 voted for on-reserve liquor

By then, everyone else had begun to move out of prohibition's shadow. Washington residents, who, like

Oregonians, drank under government control, had enjoyed highballs in lounges since 1949. In BC, liquor served by the glass remained illegal until 1952, when residents narrowly voted for it—along with teetotaller W.A.C. Bennett's new Social Credit party. BC's first cocktail lounge, a small room inside Victoria's Strathcona Hotel, was big news. On opening day, "the place was jammed until closing at 11:30 p.m." the *Daily Times* reported. It took over half a century after provincial prohibition repeal before imbibers could finally order a drink in a restaurant—although they would wait years longer to do so without ordering food—or buy a bottle on Sunday and do so from a private retailer.

In Washington and Oregon—once regarded as repressive liquor-law states—residents were buying beer and wine in food stores by the 1970s, a novel experience for BC vacationers still denied that privilege 40 years later. In 2011, Washington residents voted overwhelmingly (60-40) to make hard liquor available in grocery stores. And there was an even more significant change. Voters also told the state to end its 78-year monopoly on liquor distribution and retail. Government distribution and liquor stores were history.

In 2002, BC's government announced it would privatize liquor retailing. The plan created a furious backlash from the BC Government Employees Union (BCGEU). The government backtracked, allowing private stores but maintaining government outlets, a decision that made for decidedly unfair competition. Private retailers must buy stock from their competitor, the distribution branch (BCLDB), which operates government stores. BCLDB has the power to deny any private store its orders and to examine them to see what its competitors are selling. Private operators are denied any data at all. The government purchases inventory at a wholesale price, providing government stores with a gross profit of 80 percent. Private retailers must pay from retail price lists—in advance and with no terms. Even with a 16-percent government discount, profit margins are razor thin. This means that consumers pay higher prices in many private stores. Private stores must seek BCLDB approval for their promotional plans but have no input in BCLDB promotional plans. The BCLDB can open government liquor stores whenever and wherever it wants, without municipal bylaw approval and community consultation. Potential private operators were denied these major advantages when they applied for licences.

Convenience—not price—often determines patronage. This gives private operators the edge; they're allowed to offer consumers cold beer and wine, snack items and late-evening opening hours in convenient locations. This helps explain the early proliferation of close to 275 low-profit outlets and may also explain why, just a few months after privatization, the government stopped accepting retail licence applications. The government intends to remove this moratorium—but not until July 2022.

With a 2013 election looming and BC burdened with

a $2.5-billion deficit, Minister of Finance Kevin Falcon announced a "cost-saving" solution that included selling off "long-standing provincial holdings," including, to the public's surprise, the BCLDB and its warehouses. It was not a new notion. Thirty years after defeating a Social Credit government privatization plan, the union fought it again. Fearing union-staffed government stores would disappear, the BCGEU launched a "Don't Drop Public Liquor" public-relations campaign. However, the government's intended review of liquor regulations, including pricing, had many cheering. According to liquor-industry lawyer Mark Hicken, "genuine" wholesale pricing would be an "amazing benefit" to tourism and hospitality sectors and consumers, too, "because we'd actually have a proper competitive pricing."

Nevertheless, abandoning a profitable operation during a time of falling government revenues made little fiscal sense. Distribution branch profit for the 2011–12 fiscal year—while 8.6 percent below expectations—was still $890.4 million, a sum that would have delighted Liberal premier John Oliver, who had inaugurated government control in 1921. To sell off revenue-generating distribution for a mere fraction of a single (bad) year's profit would have rendered Oliver speechless. As Kevin Falcon stated, private operators might "manage a business much more effectively than government ever can," but arcane and contradictory regulations—including those that forbade liquor sales by grocery stores—would limit private-sector profits, too.

However, both media and public attention shifted when the opposition raised suspicions about a "highly tainted" privatization process. Lost in the ensuing rhetoric was any public debate about privatization's taxpayer benefits or its financial rationale.

While the booze battle raged, the BCGEU was renegotiating its government contract. One concept discussed was Sunday government liquor store openings. The idea was not introduced by the cash-strapped government, as one might expect, but by the union. Its president, Darryl Walker, maintained the move would generate "in excess of $100 million annually." Incredibly, government negotiators insisted the union take the issue off the table. In a statement echoing the typical rationale for many liquor decisions, Provincial Health Officer Perry Kendall maintained that "from a public health perspective, you wouldn't recommend opening more liquor stores on Sunday."

By September 2012, the government's privatization bidding process was well advanced; a short list of four bidders had been announced and the decision on a winning bidder was just a month away. Therefore, BCGEU negotiators were shocked when the government offered to cancel privatization plans in exchange for reduced BCGEU wage demands. Delighted union reps quickly agreed. After two years without raises, union workers achieved what Walker called "a decent and fair wage increase." In the flush of victory, the union also considered pressing for additional government stores and Sunday openings, further disadvantaging private retailers. One thing was clear: a 21st-century replacement for BC's 1920s-style liquor distribution monopoly was a dead issue and, retailers and hotels feared, so were changes to inconsistent liquor pricing.

"Inconsistent" is a word often used to describe the LCB's licence rulings. Along with public health, the LCB often cited "public safety," as a decision-making rationale. It used it to deny the 2011 Whistler Jazz Festival a liquor licence, except for a roped-off beer garden. Organizers argued garden licences limited financial success because minors would not be allowed to attend a family-oriented event. "What are they [the LCB] fearful of? What would this open up?" a Whistler councillor asked. "People sitting on a blanket, having wine and cheese, and listening to music; how much better can it get?" That was one side. Many event organizers experienced the other side. Drunken rowdyism in the 1980s helped destroy Vancouver's Sea Festival, Kelowna's Regatta and White Rock's Sandcastle Festival.

In January 2012, a new liquor licence appeared to be a godsend for East Vancouver's Rio Theatre, which ran films and live events. When operator Corinne Lea sat down to sign the licence agreement, she was stunned to learn that the LCB's 1920s morals-over-money mindset was still deeply entrenched. Citing "public safety," the LCB had always ruled movie theatres could not serve liquor. During screenings, darkened theatres pose "challenges . . . ensuring minors don't have access to alcohol," as Licensing Branch Manager Karen Ayers explained during what one newspaper called "The Rio Debacle." Lea was granted a licence only if the Rio stopped showing movies. Although she had just spent $120,000 for a 3-D projector and knew she would lose upcoming film-festival business, Lea reluctantly signed. Despite professional consultants' advice to passively accept the LCB's ruling, Lea hit the phone, talking to media about what she termed "hostile and punitive" licensing. She had nothing to lose: without both film and live-entertainment revenue, she knew the Rio's days were numbered.

The Rio story caused a furor. The *Vancouver Province* demanded the government "fix our liquor laws." The NDP opposition demanded the same. *Globe and Mail* readers called BC's licensing decision and liquor legislation "absolutely crazy," "paternalistic," "archaic" and "ridiculous." Another reader imagined "a pasty-faced little [government] geek sitting in a cubicle somewhere, gloating." In April 2012, the LCB announced a sudden change in licensing law: movie theatres could apply for licences. Today, moviegoers at the profitable Rio enjoy alcoholic beverages with their popcorn.

Just a month after the Rio went public, draconian retail measures were introduced to ensure private liquor retailers didn't sell liquor to minors—even by mistake. The first offence could cost a private liquor retailer as much as $7,500, or worse, the licence itself. An offending store was required to post what the LCB called a "contravention notice" revealing to patrons that the store had broken the law. Retailers called them "shaming" signs. Complained one Vancouver store manager, "There's no real reason for them to be up other than to shame us. Now we are paranoid about ID-ing."

South of the border, privately run distribution and grocery-store liquor sales won a measure of liquor peace in Washington State. Oregon residents appear ready to end their whisky wars. While the BC government was offering to scuttle liquor privatization, the *Oregonian* announced, "GROCERS TELL OREGON LAWMAKERS: UPDATE LIQUOR LAWS OR FACE INITIATIVE." Members of the Northwest Grocery Association want what Washington enjoys: private distribution and food-store shelves stocked with hard liquor. "We do believe it [distribution privatization] is coming," said association lobbyist Shawn Miller. If elected officials resist, the issue will be resolved by voters.

In BC, where even public consultation regarding distribution privatization was deemed inadequate, the province's residents haven't been able to vote on a liquor issue since 1952. Consequently, BC continues to linger in prohibition's shadow. Despite some relaxation of public drinking laws, including a clumsy private/government retail system, the province's liquor legislation harkens back to 1921's Liquor Act—now a patchwork of enforcement amendments and contradictory and anachronistic regulations. Under such a system, BC's whisky wars are likely far from over.

Selected Bibliography

Books

Blumenthal, Ralph. *Stork Club*. Boston: Little, Brown & Company, 2000.

Campbell, Robert A. *Demon Rum or Easy Money: Government Control of Liquor in British Columbia, from Prohibition to Privatization.* Ottawa: Carleton University Press, 1991.

———. "A 'Fantastic Rigmarole': Deregulating Aboriginal Drinking in British Columbia, 1945–62." *BC Studies* 141 (Spring 2004): 81–104.

———. "Liquor and Liberals: Patronage and Government Control in British Columbia, 1920–1928." *BC Studies* 77 (Spring 1988): 30–53.

Clark, Norman H. *The Dry Years: Prohibition and Social Change in Washington.* Seattle: University of Washington Press, 1988.

Green, Ruth. *Personality Ships of British Columbia*. Vancouver: Marine Tapestry Publications, 1969.

Hamilton, Douglas L. *Sobering Dilemma: A History of Prohibition in British Columbia.* Vancouver: Ronsdale Press, 2004.

Metcalfe, Phillip. *Whispering Wires: The Tragic Tale of an American Bootlegger.* Portland, OR: Inkwater Press, 2007.

Miles, Fraser. *Slow Boat on Rum Row*. Madeira Park, BC: Harbour Publishing, 1992.

Newsome, Eric. *The Case of the Beryl G*. Victoria: Orca Book Publishers, 1989.

Parker, Marion, and Robert Tyrell. *Rumrunner: The Life and Times of Johnny Schnarr.* Victoria: Orca Book Publishers, 1988.

Stonier-Newman, Lynne. *Policing a Pioneer Province: The BC Provincial Police 1858–1950.* Madeira Park, BC: Harbour Publishing, 1991.

Newspapers

Oregonian (Portland, OR).

Port Townsend Daily Leader.

Seattle Times.

Vancouver Daily World.

Vancouver Province.

Vancouver Sun.

Unpublished Sources

Hiebert, Albert John. *Prohibition in B.C.* Master's thesis. Waterloo University College, 1963.

LaMar, Ryan. *Prohibition in Portland and Oregon.* Unpublished paper. Washington State University, 2005.

Price, Ruth. *The Politics of Liquor in British Columbia: 1920–1928.* Master's thesis. Simon Fraser University, 1979.

Websites

BreweryGems. www.brewerygems.com

HistoryLink. www.historylink.org

University of Washington Libraries Digital Collections. http://content.lib.washington.edu

Special thanks are extended to Russ Hanbey of Seattle, descendant of police officer and bootleg victim Sergeant John Weedin, and to the Rio Theatre's irrepressible liquor-law change agent, Corinne Lea.

Index

About the Author

The prolific author of over a dozen Amazing Stories, Rich Mole lives in Calgary, Alberta. *Rum-Runners and Renegades* is the second book of a comprehensive two-volume history of liquor on the West Coast. The first volume, *Scoundrels and Saloons*, covers the years from 1840 to 1917. Among Rich's other Amazing Stories are *Whisky Wars of the Canadian West, Dirty Thirties Desperadoes, The Chilcotin War, Rebel Women of the West Coast, Rebel Women of the Klondike* and *Gold Fever*.

Rich welcomes emails at ramole@telus.net.

More Amazing Stories by Rich Mole

Scoundrels and Saloons

Whisky Wars of the Pacific Northwest
1840–1917

print ISBN 978-1-927051-78-8
ebook ISBN 978-1-927051-79-5

Between 1840 and 1917, the battle over liquor was
a constant thread weaving through the history of
the Pacific Northwest. Rich Mole brings to life a
cast of murderous liquor traders, angry Natives,
corrupt policemen and politicians, and zealous
prohibitionists in this complete and compelling
account of the struggles for and against having a
drink in frontier BC, Washington and Oregon.

Dirty Thirties Desperadoes

Forgotten Victims of the Great Depression

print ISBN 978-1-926613-95-6
ebook ISBN 978-1-926936-64-2

In October 1935, three Doukhobor farm boys
embarked on a violent trail of robbery and murder
that stretched from Manitoba to Alberta. By the
time the spree ended, the fugitives and four lawmen
were dead. This gripping narrative reveals surprising
new details about the tragic events as it chronicles
the disastrous impact of the Great Depression on the
young killers and those who faced them down.

Purchase Amazing Stories at your favourite bookstore
or visit heritagehouse.ca to order online.

RUM-RUNNERS
AND RENEGADES

Whisky Wars of the Pacific Northwest, 1917–2012

RICH MOLE

VICTORIA · VANCOUVER · CALGARY

Heritage House Publishing Company Ltd.
heritagehouse.ca

Library and Archives Canada Cataloguing in Publication
Mole, Rich, 1946–
     Rum-runners and renegades: whisky wars of the Pacific Northwest, 1917-2012 / Rich Mole.

(Amazing stories)
Includes bibliographical references and index.
Also issued in electronic format.
ISBN 978-1-927527-25-2

1. Temperance—Northwest, Pacific—History—20th century. 2. Prohibition—Northwest, Pacific—History—20th century. 3. Northwest, Pacific—Biography. I. Title. II. Series: Amazing stories (Victoria, B.C.)

HV5309.B7M643 2013   363.4'109795   C2013-900029-1

Series editor: Lesley Reynolds
Proofreader: Liesbeth Leatherbarrow

Cover photo: A member of Seattle's dry squad destroys a fermenting vat in a bootlegger's 65th Avenue hideaway. University of Washington Special Collections, PH Coll 676.8, Prohibition Era/Matt Starwich Collection, UW22113.

MIX
Paper from
responsible sources
FSC
www.fsc.org   FSC® C016245

The interior of this book was produced on 30% post-consumer recycled paper, processed chlorine free and printed with vegetable-based inks.

Heritage House acknowledges the financial support for its publishing program from the Government of Canada through the Canada Book Fund (CBF), Canada Council for the Arts and the province of British Columbia through the British Columbia Arts Council and the Book Publishing Tax Credit.

 Canadian Patrimoine
Heritage canadien

 Canada Council   Conseil des Arts
for the Arts   du Canada

 BRITISH COLUMBIA
ARTS COUNCIL

17 16 15 14 13 1 2 3 4 5
Printed in Canada